SUPERMAN
Doesn't Live
Here Anymore

SUPERMAN
Doesn't Live Here Anymore

Drugs Are a Lie,
Jesus Is the Truth

by Scott McPhillips

Mac on the Attack for Jesus
Honey Creek, IA

Although the author and publisher have made every effort to ensure the accuracy and completeness of information contained in this book, we assume no responsibility for errors, inaccuracies, omissions, or any inconsistency herein. Any slights of people, places, or organizations are unintentional.

First printing 1998
Second printing 1999

ISBN 0-9662205-4-4 (Hardcover)
ISBN 0-9662205-7-9 (Softcover)

LCCN 98-65353

ATTENTION SPORTS ORGANIZATIONS, CORPORATIONS, UNIVERSITIES, COLLEGES, AND PROFESSIONAL ORGANIZATIONS: Quantity discounts are available on bulk purchases of this book for educational purposes. Special books or book excerpts can also be created to fit specific needs. For information, please contact Mac on the Attack for Jesus, 28535 Coldwater Avenue, Honey Creek, IA 51542, phone (712) 545-3003.

CONTENTS

Where to now, St. Peter?
If it's true, I'm in your hands.
I may not be a Christian,
But I've done all one man can.

I understand I'm on the road
Where all that was is gone,
So where to now, St. Peter?
Show me which road I'm on,
Which road I'm on.

—Bernie Taupin, *Where to Now, St. Peter?*
Knopf Publishing, 1976

Special K

by Gaylord Schelling

WRITTEN JULY 1991

Gaylord Schelling is the high school football coach in Atlantic, Iowa. Before he moved to Atlantic, Gaylord coached Scott at Tri-Center High School in Neola, Iowa. Coach Schelling's admiration for Scott grew into a friendship that continues today.

A few years ago, Coach Schelling attended a writer's workshop. There, he was challenged by various assignments designed to sharpen his written communication skills. One of those assignments motivated him to write about Scott. The following piece outlines Scott's story, which is an affirmation of the value of life itself and the strength of human will.

■ ■ ■ ■ ■

Scott Krumwiede (who now goes by the name Scott McPhillips) was the best athlete I have ever coached. He was an all-state player in football, basketball, and baseball. He was not, however, the stereotypical all-star athlete. Many athletes shy away from pressure plays, but Scott thrived on them. He loved having the ball during crucial game situations. Scott was a leader both emotionally and physically. He worked very hard in practice and did whatever it took to become great. Probably his best quality was that he never quit, no matter what the score was. Scott amazed me with his ability to come through with the play to win the game.

Like all great people, he had faults. Scott had trouble with drinking and other drugs. We fought and argued over his alcohol abuse. I threatened him and became very frustrated with his lack of self-discipline in this area of his life. Still, no matter how hard I tried, I couldn't get my point about drug abuse through to him.

During Scott's freshman year in college, he had his first automobile accident involving alcohol. He suffered a broken arm and some facial lacerations. After the accident, Scott came to speak to one of my seventh grade classes. He meant well, but he couldn't turn the corner with his alcohol problem. He dropped out of Simpson College, even though he had a good start on his college athletic career. He had started at free safety in football and had pitched some varsity baseball.

A year and a half later, Scott was thinking about going back to Simpson. His mother was looking forward to his return to college.

Then in October 1989, he hit another car head on. The driver of the other car was killed. Scott was trapped in his car for two and a half hours before he was found. He was in surgery for ten hours and suffered unbelievable injuries to all parts of his body except for vital internal organs.

A year and a half later, Scott had undergone numerous surgeries on his arms and legs. This past weekend, he walked into my house for the first time without the aid of a wheelchair or support. Scott still does not remember his great athletic accomplishments, but he has not lost his ability to fight. Few doctors thought he would live, let alone walk and recover the use of his arms or legs. He had to relearn how to speak. Scott's will to "never say never" is his strength.

Now Scott wants to tell his story. He knows he had a problem. He knows he will never be what he once was. It has been a struggle for Scott to learn about life the hard way. He realizes he still has a big battle ahead. Scott has learned a lot, and he wants to let kids know what he has learned and to share the miracle of his recovery. He would like kids to realize there are ways to cope when the struggles of life seem too great without abusing alcohol and drugs.

Life has a purpose; believe it!

ACKNOWLEDGMENTS

I owe so much thanks to so many people, it would take a book at least this big to list them all and what they've done for me.

Always hovering in the background since I was born: Grandmother and Grandfather. They've always been up front when I needed love and support, and have been with me either physically or spiritually all the time. I love both of you very much.

My special thanks to my good friend and mentor, Bob Darrah, whose guidance and encouragement are priceless. A smart man with an abundance of ideas, he always made time to help me grow. He's a great planner and has shown me how to get things done. His confidence in me gives me strength.

Thanks to Bill Henjum, my speech coach. Bill worked with me every weekday for about five months, while this book was being written, to help me speak more clearly to individuals and to groups.

Thanks, too, to my new friend, George Kaywood, whose way with words has helped me to tell my story just the way I want it to be told. He became my confidant during the writing of this book, and I very much appreciate his trust. He made sure every detail was accurate and easy to understand.

Thanks to my mother, Beverly Krumwiede, for her abundant love and endless faith in me (a mother is a special friend); my brother, Steve McPhillips (we had our differences, but I love you); and to Gaylord Schelling, for his direction and support and for being the best coach I ever had.

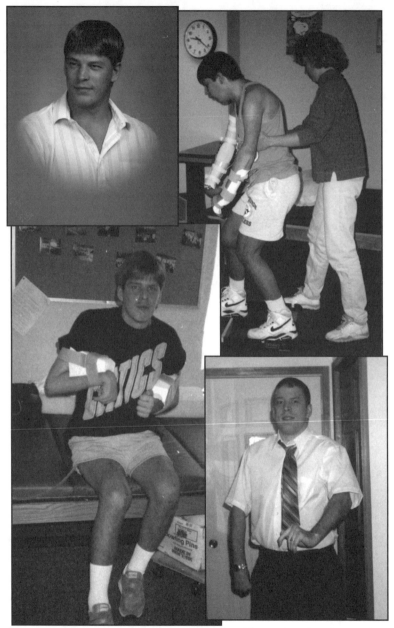

Top left: *Just before the accident.* ***Top right:*** *16 months after the accident. Getting closer to walking on my own.* ***Bottom left:*** *8 months after the accident. Finally able to sit up by myself.* ***Bottom right:*** *It's Mac on the Attack for Jesus. The new man.*

It was October 10 when my world changed forever and my life came to a temporary halt. I was on a gravel road in rural Iowa. Drunk and high on drugs, I was driving fast and loose when I approached the crest of a hill. I crashed head on into another car, killing its driver who was also my brother's best friend, Robert Thomas. He was twenty-four years old.

I wish I could describe the accident in great detail and use vivid, graphic descriptions to unsettle you. But I can't because I just don't remember.

It was 1989 when I had the accident. It was 1990 when I woke up. Nine months of my life had vanished. What is nine months? It may not seem like a very long time, but when you're barely out of your teens, it's something akin to forever. Nine months is almost an entire year of school. It's thirty-nine weekends. I missed Thanksgiving. Christmas. New Year's Day. Easter. The Fourth of July. My twenty-first birthday. My life came to a screeching halt, never to be the same again.

Beginnings

My mother says I've been giving people grief ever since the day I was born. I've been strong-willed and impatient all my life, beginning with my entrance into the world during the first winter storm of the season in November 1968. Mom barely made it to the hospital to deliver me.

I grew into a stubborn boy prone to temper tantrums. One of my earliest memories was when I was in second grade and put into "jail." Jail meant I had to leave the classroom and could not come back until I was given permission. After I left the building (with my teacher keeping a close eye on me), I peeked into the classroom window. The other students had been prompted to jeer, and they yelled, "Get away, jailbird! No peeking!" I played on the playground swings for a while but soon grew tired of my unstructured freedom. I quietly snuck back into the school, found a comfortable spot on the floor of the library, and went to sleep. The teacher became alarmed when I vanished from her sight. After a brief search, I was discovered. That was pretty much the end of it, but it was the first of many incidents where Mom was proven right about my ability to give everyone grief.

Frequently, I announced I was running away from home. Mom would say, "Okay," and pack some food. She also made sure I wore something that could be easily spotted, such as a red or orange jacket. Obviously, this type of response makes the decision to run worthless as an attention-getting tactic. I would leave, walk a bit, go behind a tree, then turn around and check to see if anyone was following. Of course, I always went back home. But I did this over and over until it finally dawned on me that it just wasn't any good.

For as long as I can remember, I've been interested in sports. Like many young boys, I wanted to be a professional athlete. The inspiration to excel at sports

When not pitching, I was catching. PeeWee Baseball. Coach Jay Anderson.

was fueled by my brother Steve's success. He was an outstanding quarterbackat Neola Tri- Center High School in Iowa before he graduated in 1983. But as much as I admired him, I always wanted to be better than him. And I was.

Most people work hard at developing athletic ability, and some are fortunate enough to be born with a natural predisposition to excel at sports. I was one of the latter types. When I was as young as twelve or thirteen, I played ball with older kids because I was good. I remember enjoying this acceptance by my "elders" and wishing I was older. I practiced to make sure my ball-playing ability would keep me in the company of "the big kids."

Children who have this natural athletic ability are both blessed and cursed. When kids as young as seventh or eighth grade play team sports in school, their coaches try to instill in them the spirit of teamwork. And when one of those students displays superior ability, a coach will always let that student know he or she is better than the rest. This message is sometimes subtle but can never be completely hidden from the rest of the team. The manner of speaking between a coach and the star player sometimes takes on a much different manner than talks to the entire team. I know this because I lived it. As a result, I developed quite an ego at an early age.

When I was out on the playing field, however, I was always willing to do whatever was necessary to help my teammates and coaches. I was a bruiser, but I was a team player. I loved playing football. Sports was my life. Between football seasons, I spent my time playing basketball and baseball. My confidence and pride both skyrocketed when I was named all-state in all three sports.

In high school, sports proficiency is often equivalent to social status or popularity. Students, teachers, family, and townspeople all fed my ego day in and day out. I had a seemingly endless supply of affection and admiration. I was a well-liked, mighty figure who brought recognition and standing to his school and community.

I was a good student who had bad habits. When I think back, I am amazed I was able to make the honor roll. I skipped a lot of school because I was too tired or too hung over. I enjoyed only a few subjects. Because I found these interesting, I paid attention in class and was able to skate through without even taking notes. I passed those courses by being able to recall just enough information for exams, probably in much the same way people who are passionate about certain interests are able to remember almost everything they learn about what they love. Friends did my homework for me in the courses I didn't like. Girls especially were eager to impress me, and I took advantage of them. Some were always willing to keep class notes for me or prep me for exams. I thought I was so smart. I thought I knew everything.

Yes, I had it all. Fame. Success. Love. An easy lifestyle. Hopes for a fabulous future. But I wanted even more. I was being consumed by a lust that would soon start me to lead another kind of life. A life that would almost kill me.

Temptation

I can't remember exactly how or when I began using drugs, but it was some time in junior high school. No one had to coerce me into trying dope. I was Big Man on Campus, but I wanted to be even more cool and more popular. I wanted to experience everything that looked fun and exciting. Thanks to my popularity in school, I was given drugs for free by so-called friends who wanted to hang around with me. I liked the high I got from marijuana. I thought I could handle it.

My life soon revolved around sports, women, alcohol, and drugs, usually in that order. Booze, grass, pills, coke, acid—I did it all with one exception: I'm happy to say I never stuck a needle into my arm. I've seen others do it, but no matter how high I ever got or wanted to get, if someone offered me a needle, I always refused. I never needed to get off that badly.

Some people were surprised drugs were as accessible in a small Iowa town as in a big city. The situation was wide open during the eighties. If you wanted it, you could get it. At first, transactions were done away from school, but once you proved you were skillful enough to buy, store, and use drugs cleverly enough so no one suspected anything, deals went down on the school grounds as well.

In junior high, I only did drugs at night, away from school property and away from home. I was able to conceal my drug use from everyone, including my family. I made up excuses as to my whereabouts. I would say I was "going out with friends," "going on a date," or some other reason that never aroused suspicion. Because I got away with it, my ego was fed even more. I was successful at everything I wanted to do. The cocky little boy was king.

During my high school years, I became a heavy drug user. I did drugs every morning, every night, and whenever else I could. The more I took, the more I wanted to reach a higher high. My state of mind was "gimme, gimme, gimme!"

I remember going into my world geography class every day higher than a kite because I did drugs before class. I remember playing in a football game with a vial of cocaine in my hip pocket. I thought using coke would improve my game. It never dawned on me that some of my best games were played without drugs.

Soon, the drugs I got for free were not enough, and I became a regular buyer when freebies weren't available. It was just the cost of having fun. I worked my way into the network of people who bought and sold drugs. I became a small-time dealer—not to make money but to earn enough cash to cover my own habit. I was able to support my own desires comfortably thanks to the number of willing buyers I met in school.

I may have fooled my family, but I wasn't able to fool my friends. My own inner circle of friends (real friends, not the ones who did drugs with me and saw nothing wrong with it) could see I was into drugs and tried to stop me. They didn't preach but they made it clear they wanted me to stop. They tried many times to convince me I was hurting myself. No one, including the girls who were doing my homework and trying to impress me, could make me listen. I thought—and said—"Get away from me! I'm on top of the world!"

And on top of the world I stayed, becoming more and more confident I would never fall. I had everything I wanted in life, and it looked like there was even more to come.

Good Times, Bad Times

Mr. Tough Guy (Maniac).

Knowing you're good and not letting it go to your head is one of the most difficult things in the world for anyone—especially a kid—to master. Sure, there were hours of practice, drills, pep talks, all the things that big school athletes need to become winners. For me it was not work but a lot of fun.

My school (Tri-Center High School) went to the state level of competition in football, basketball, and baseball for the 1985–1986 school year. We placed second in both basketball and baseball—not bad for a small school in a small Iowa farm town. The following year, I was selected as an all-state athlete in all three

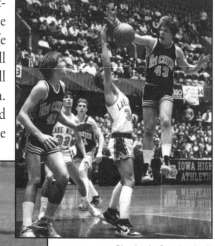

Sky high for the ball.

Ready to hurl a 94 mph fast ball.

sports. My goal of becoming a professional athlete seemed to be getting closer.

Tri-Center captured the Iowa State Baseball Championship in 1987. I pitched a good game and even hit a home run the first time I came to bat. I was also named the game's most valuable player. Or so I've been told. Because of my accident, I cannot remember the greatest accomplishments of my sports career.

Being interviewed by press after winning the state championship.

In fall 1987, I was eighteen years old and just starting to trade adolescence for adulthood. I enrolled in Simpson College in Indianola, Iowa. Simpson was only a couple of hours away from home, but far enough away from any restrictions you have to observe when living with your family. When I made the move from Honey Creek to Indianola, drugs moved with me. I quickly learned how to contact the "right" people and found they were like everyone else I'd met in high school: It was a big deal for them to supply and do drugs with the star athlete.

Life at the men-only dorm Barker Hall was one big party. My sports skills cemented my image as Big Man on Campus. I had four different girlfriends vying for my affection. I kept my grades just strong enough to stay out of academic trouble. And the drug pipeline was open and working.

Then on Wednesday night, October 22, 1987, a friend and I were headed east on Interstate 80, returning to Indianola after partying in Des Moines. We were both high, driving fast in my brother's new black sports car, which I had borrowed for a few days. No one knows how the accident happened. All that is definite is that the car hit a guardrail. I must have thought I was in trouble because the first thing I did when I heard the wail of police sirens was to run. I'm told I ran

What's left of the car.

across the interstate, put my broken arm on a fencepost, jumped over the fence, and hollered back at my friend, "Good-bye! See ya tomorrow!"

I have a hazy memory of running along a set of railroad tracks, falling on some cinders, and seeing a broken bone sticking out of my arm. The police radioed for a medical helicopter, and it's a good thing they did. The searchlight on the helicopter spotted me lying on the ground after I had passed out. The last thing I remember is being helped by some policemen. Then darkness.

The luck that seemed to be a natural part of my life was still with me. Whoever witnessed or came upon the accident must have reported it quickly. I was pretty banged up, and if there had been much of a delay, I might not have lived. I was rushed to the hospital in Des Moines. After it was determined how much surgery I would need for my injuries, one of the two specialists who would have to operate on me coincidentally happened to be in Des Moines at the time.

My left forearm was fractured. Compound. The doctors had to fit a steel plate on what was left to hold it together. It's still there today. Unless you touched my arm, you'd never known how mangled it was. Of course, you don't want to touch my arm, because the feel of steel under live skin is so unusual, it's enough to spook just about anybody.

My face was cracked open when it hit the steering wheel, requiring seventy- two stitches on the outside and another seventy-two stitches on the inside. The stitches

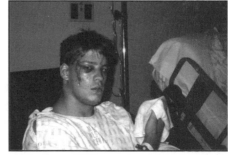

Pretty boy?

ran from my right eye halfway down to my chin. Again, I was lucky—my face healed without producing any ugly scars, but I've still got a couple of permanent hash marks to remind me of that night every time I look into a mirror. And believe it or not, the only thing I was worried about at the time was if the girls would still be attracted to me in spite of an ugly scar on my face! I told myself the scar would make me look tougher, more macho, so maybe it wasn't that bad after all.

I have no doubt today this accident was a warning from God. He was trying to show me what my real friends had been trying to tell me: I was throwing my life away and headed for serious trouble if I kept living a drug-based lifestyle. Had I heeded God's warning, the big fall that followed might never have happened.

I didn't listen. My ego continued to get stroked. When I was in high school, I made sports headlines regularly and thrived on it. Kevin White, a writer for *The Daily Nonpareil* in Council Bluffs, Iowa, wrote these words during my rehabilitation. At the time, I felt it was one of the highest compliments I ever received.

Going up for two.

…And this is a guy who was not your everyday athlete. He was flat gifted. People said he couldn't play the post position in basketball at 5-foot-10. But his senior year, he was simply unstoppable, averaging 25.7 points and 11.3 rebounds a game. The scoring average was easily the best ever for one season at Tri-Center. He also ended up as the sixth best rebounder in T-C [Tri-Center High School] history.

Whatever he lacked in height, he more than made up for in pure effort. When you got in a game he'd find a way to beat you.

...(Scott was)...unquestionably one of the best athletes the school has ever produced.

■ ■ ■ ■ ■

I healed quickly. But my playing days on the football field were over. It would be impossible for me to play football with a steel plate in my arm. My doctor added that with the head injury I had sustained, one good hit or body slam and...well, it's not a pretty picture.

In addition to the depressing realization I could never play football again, I couldn't swing a baseball bat very well because of the injuries to my arm. My baseball career was on hold indefinitely. In addition, I didn't like my baseball coach, John Siriani, because he was always on my back to study and improve my grades. Now I realize he was right, I was wrong, and he has become a friend. I quickly lost interest in Simpson College and decided I had no reason to stay in Indianola. I dropped out of Simpson and returned home with plans to enroll in Iowa Western Community College in nearby Council Bluffs. Iowa Western had a pretty good baseball team, and I thought I could play baseball once I got there.

I started classes during the 1988–1989 term, but true to form, I concentrated on fun and games rather than getting a degree. I don't remember much of the time I spent there, but I failed every class. I managed to play a little baseball there but did nothing noteworthy. The assistant coach, Kevin Whitehall, said I was a good person but had some bad habits. What an understatement! I still couldn't see how much success and opportunity I had thrown away or how I was continuing to destroy my life.

The Big Sleep

After an accident as damaging as the first one I had, it's amazing I didn't change my lifestyle. I should have gotten the message I'd better change my ways to make sure something like that would never happen again. But even after the pain of my corrective surgery, the awful realization I couldn't play football anymore, and the awareness that my chances of becoming a professional athlete were slim or none, it was still party time.

That is, until that fateful night in October 1989, when my world came crashing down around me, and I fell off the top of the world.

While I was in that nine-month coma my sports career came to an end. My education stopped. My prestige and popularity faded away. My girlfriends, concerned at first, drifted away. My friends grew distant. My growth as a human being was put on hold. "Out of sight, out of mind" is true. Time pushes things away—people, pain, emotions, even values. During my nine months of being out of sight, literally and figuratively, my entire life changed. I can only blame myself. I lived carelessly. I let my ego dictate my actions, never for a moment considering the consequences.

I don't remember anything during that period of time. I thank God for the faith and courage of my mother, Beverly Krumwiede. Fortunately, she had the presence of mind and the strength to write down what happened and her thoughts and the decisions she had to make for me. Here's what she wrote:

■ ■ ■ ■ ■

It began for me with a phone call at one in the morning. "Your son is being life-flighted to St. Joseph's Hospital in Omaha. I suggest you get there as soon as possible."

After I reached the hospital, I rushed into the emergency room. There were so many doctors and nurses surrounding Scott that I couldn't even see him. They let me talk to him at 3:00 A.M., as they were wheeling him to surgery. They thought he might be able to hear me.

Scott required many operations. The doctors were extremely nice and caring, as they came out between each round of surgery, explaining what they had done and were going to do next. For example: (1) placed a rod in the left femur, which had been broken in four or five places; (2) fixed the right knee; (3) put in an external pelvic apparatus to correct the pelvic bones that had been pulled four inches apart, causing a small puncture in the bladder; and (4) put screws in the right foot to fix the broken talus bone.

The surgery ended at 1:00 P.M. the next afternoon. It had taken ten hours for the doctors to finish their work. There was a lapse of four hours from the accident itself, which happened at 9:15 P.M., until Scott got to the hospital. He was not found for two and a half hours, and then it took over an hour to get him out of the car.

I was not ready for the shock of seeing Scott in intensive care. A blue wire was attached to his head, actually connected through the scalp to his brain, to monitor brain pressure. A tube protruded up and out of his right lung, which had been punctured and deflated in the accident. His right leg was in a cast. He had a respirator to help him breathe.

Scott developed a fever. 105 degrees. At one point, his breathing suddenly became faster and shallower. Pneumonia in the left lung. Another tube. Another machine.

So many machines. So many "beeps" and screaming-type sounds. At least that's what they sounded like to me. I was petrified whenever a warning signal sounded. Each one triggered the same thought: "My God, he's going to die and no one is running in here to help him!"

After the hospital staff explained what each sound meant, the panic went away. I hope that hospital care personnel everywhere ex-

plain what all the machines are, and what all the sounds mean as soon as possible to parents unfortunate enough to go through what I did. It will help them a lot.

I'll always be thankful for all the information the hospital staff at St. Joseph's gave to me personally. It doesn't matter how much printed information you're given. After an accident like the one Scott was in, you're simply not in a state of mind to comprehend much of what you read.

One bit of advice I'm especially thankful for was, "The more you are with him and can talk to him, the better and faster he will come out of it." I think I'll always be remembered at St. Joseph's as the Mom who read and talked to her son all but the last ten minutes of every two hours in intensive care.

Scott was in intensive care at St. Joseph's for 26 days. He was moved to the rehabilitation section of Immanuel Medical Center in Omaha on December 5, 1989.

In February 1990, I moved Scott to Independence, Missouri, to continue his treatment as an inpatient in a program that specialized in people with head-injuries. At this time, Scott's left arm and hand had too much muscle tone. It had twisted so that if you didn't keep a pillow at his elbow, he could choke himself. His right arm had little or no muscle tone, and was drawn up with his hand dropped. His right leg was drawn up, and his shoulders and body were starting to draw up into a fetal position.

■ ■ ■ ■ ■

I did not learn about Rob's death for a long time after the fatal crash. During my rehabilitation, I was able to go home on weekends. On one of those visits, my mother took me to a baseball game where I saw Rob Thomas's older brother. Unaware Rob had died in the crash, I said something half-jokingly about Rob to him. He looked at me oddly and said, "You don't know what happened," and walked away. I still feel bad about having to wait so long to find out.

Seeing how puzzled I was, Mom asked my psychologist about telling me the truth. He told her she could decide when to tell me based on how she thought I would handle it. She chose to tell me while we were staying in Kansas City one weekend near the complex where I was undergoing rehabilitation. The psychologist would be close by if I needed help. As I lay on the bed in our motel room, she told me that on the night of the accident, my car had not hit a tree as I had been told earlier.

"You met a car head on at the crest of a hill," she said quietly.

"Who was in the other car?" I asked.

"Rob Thomas."

"How is Rob?" I asked with a sense of foreboding.

"Rob is in heaven with God." She looked at me. "God has called Rob home. All of our days are numbered, you know."

I didn't know what to say. I couldn't believe it. I lay there in silence, rolling the realization over and over in my mind. What could I possibly have said that would have made any sense after hearing I had killed someone?

I think about Rob's death every day. It's like a knife sticking through my heart. Is there any way to ever put aside the knowledge you caused another person to lose his life because of your own stupidity?

There are times today when I find it hard to believe I've actually been through all this. I don't feel sorry for myself, however, because I know it's all part of God's plan for me. It's a terribly hard way to learn a simple lesson, but had it not been for the accident, I probably would never have learned what's really important in life.

The Awakening

Just what is a coma?

The dictionary defines it as "a state of deep unconsciousness, caused by disease, injury, or poison." But this is not necessarily accurate. Most people think you're either in a coma or not in a coma—completely unconscious or completely awake. According to Dr. Gene Rankin, a neuropsychologist at Immanuel Medical Center in Omaha, Nebraska, there are various degrees of comas. One type (usually represented in the movies) is deep and extreme. People in this type of coma do not respond to or feel pain. People in a near-coma seem to be awake but are unaware of what is going on around you. And there are gradations between those two extremes.

According to medical reports, I went through many different coma stages. While I was at St. Joseph's, I gave no response to questions or to pain. After moving to Immanuel, although I still couldn't talk, I blinked my eyes once or twice in response to "yes" and "no" questions. (Dr. Rankin says eye blink tests, however, are not considered reliable because it's hard to get consistent results. Some say I was consistent. Take your pick.) And in Independence, I continued the eye blinks, started to nod my head, and so on. At least, that's what I'm told.

It wasn't until July 1990 that I really woke up, opened my eyes, and was able to think, "Where am I? What's going on here?" I had been on various medications that were supposed to help me reach this "normal" level of awareness and had very recently had an operation. Sometimes the effect of an operation combined with medications and other conditions can trigger an awakening from a coma. Whatever triggered it, I was "back."

The moment I opened my eyes I knew something was wrong. Fear gripped me. My hands and arms were crossed and I couldn't move them. In fact, I couldn't move much of my body at all having had the unconscious tendency to scrunch up into a fetal position so much. At first I thought I had taken some contaminated drugs. Maybe I was on some crazy type of a bad trip.

Then, a moment or two later, I thought I was at home. I tried to yell out, "Mom!" Alerted by the half-formed sounds I made, the first words anyone had heard me utter in months, two nurses came rushing in.

"Do you know where you are?" one asked.

Confused, I mouthed, "No."

"You're in the hospital, " one nurse told me.

An overdose, I thought to myself. I did too many drugs this time and wound up overdosing.

The nurses' short explanation hit me like a bullet: "You were in an accident and you've been in a coma for nine months."

What's left of my car.

It was impossible to comprehend the full meaning of those few words. I tried to ask questions, as if a survival reflex had been tweaked. I wanted and needed information.

I couldn't talk. I wanted to say, "Where's my mother? I want to talk to Mom," but I must have uttered something like, "Muhhhh?"

"Your mother's not here right now, but she'll be very happy to know you've come out of your coma. She'll be here this weekend."

I tried to ask, "Where's my brother?" I didn't hear the answer. As I listened to my own words, I thought, "My God! My speech is so slurred! I can't believe how bad I sound! I can hardly make a sound!"

One of the nurses asked me, "Do you know what year it is?"

I thought to myself, "Sure. It's 1989."

"It's 1990, Scott."

Nineteen-ninety. My life had stopped before I was able to turn the calendar. I was still in 1989.

Why couldn't I remember what happened? I tried, but I could not recall any details of that terrible night…and I still can't remember to this day. Was my mind blocking out the awful sounds, smells, and pain of my own massive wounds, as well as the death of my brother's best friend? Was it part of the head injury that affected my speech and ability to move? Or, most likely, a little bit of both?

My disbelief at what was happening was pushed aside for the moment by the announcement that I had undergone surgery on my right leg. I tried my best to ask why I had needed the surgery.

"So you'll be able to walk," was the simple explanation.

I thought, "Ridiculous! Me, an all-state sports star, needing surgery to walk. Of course I can walk!"

I wanted to tell them I didn't need a wheelchair. I knew I could walk. I would show them.

But of course I couldn't get up. My nurses smiled at me. They were so happy I had come out of my coma after nine months that my "cocky little boy" attitude made no difference.

It's always a big deal—often rightfully called a miracle—when someone comes out of a coma. Soon after I awoke, doctors and nurses hurried into and out of the room, or so it seemed to me. Although they quickly told me where I was and how I had arrived there, I had a very difficult time trying to understand what my mind was doing in this really screwed-up body.

Soon after the uproar died down, I learned I was at Rebound, a unit of the Independence Regional Health Center in Independence, Missouri. Rebound specialized in patients with head injuries who needed extensive therapy both physically and mentally if they were to lead what most people would call normal lives. Mom had decided it would be the best place for me. (I use the past tense in describing Rebound, because after I left, HealthSouth Rehabilitation Corporation bought the center and Rebound is officially known today as the Kansas City Rehabilitation Network.)

I am indebted to the people at Rebound. They are responsible for my rebirth.

My life at Rebound was a combination of introspection, physical and mental exercise, discovery, and learning. Rehabilitation at Rebound was divided into two parts: first, time spent as an in-patient; later, living by yourself on the grounds as part of the transition back to life outside an environment of structured care. Not only did I need different types of therapy to regain the ability to walk, reason, and simply use my body the way most people take for granted, I had to relearn many simple tasks ranging from bathroom habits to dressing myself.

When I began my stay as an in-patient at Rebound, someone told me what the day and date were before I went to sleep every night. When I got up the next morning, I could not remember either. Occasionally, I would even forget where my room was.

For a long part of my stay at Rebound as an in-patient, someone had to dress me every morning—and change my diapers! I had to wear them because I could not communicate to anyone when I had to use the toilet. I didn't have any control of my bladder at that time because my brain was not sending messages to my body for various functions that require your mind and body to work together. And when you gotta go, you gotta go. It was incredibly degrading to be aware of what was happening but having no control over it.

For about two years, I had to wear special brace-like devices when I went to bed at night. I became very frustrated when I had to wait for help to get into and out of bed every day. In the hospital, you have to learn to wait your turn, but the need to have someone always helping you aggravates even slight discomforts.

If you can, think back to when you were a small child. Do you remember how many times you tried to get a button through a buttonhole? Trying over and over again to tie your shoes? If that takes you too far back, then think about when you first learned to ride a bicycle. How many times did you wobble, fall off, get up, and do it again before you learned what the proper balance should feel like?

That's what it was like for me, except I already knew what should happen, how the simple routines of daily life worked and how they should feel. But I couldn't do them. I had to learn like a child does. The learning process was repetitive, slow, and very frustrating.

The person who did the most for me was Mom. She made the 222-mile trip from her house to Rebound every weekend to pick me up so I could be home with family and friends. She would pick me up at Rebound, take me home for a couple of days, then take me back to Rebound on Sunday night. That's 888 miles every weekend!

These weekly road trips became as much a part of my therapy

Above: Home with my pets. Trying to make my arms move to pet the cat.

Right: Home after first surgery with friend. Biggest smile I could get. Notice my hands.

as the more formal routines at Rebound. I discovered I could talk to Mom about anything. If I ever got out of line, she'd let me know about it. If she said I was wrong about something, I later realized I was really wrong. The practice of talking about and listening to ideas and the events that had happened in my life helped to shape the values I have today. I'm sure it was tiring for her, but it was an important part of rebuilding my life.

Mom continued to keep a journal, and the notes she made while I was at Rebound tell some stories worth sharing. Here's part of her journal from that time:

■　■　■　■　■

The first weekend I drove to Independence to see Scott, I was very upset to see him sitting in a wheelchair with a padded board behind his back for support. He had to be strapped in, with straps over his shoulders to hold him up. The therapists explained to me, "When you put yourself at a sharp 90-degree angle, what do you feel? It's a message to your brain. Relax and put yourself in a reclining position, and what do you feel? Nothing."

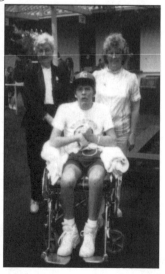

I remember watching Rebound staff members struggling with Scott just to get him from his bed to a chair. His feet always hit the floor. They said to me, "Stomp your feet on the floor. What do you feel? It's a message to your brain!" They were trying to get Scott's brain to receive messages and make his body respond to them.

Every weekend, there was some little bit of improvement: Scott's nodding his head "yes," shaking it side to side for "no," shrugging his shoulders, moving the wheelchair backwards, and later pulling it forward, first with both feet and eventually with one foot after

Mother's Day 1990. Grandma, Mom and Scott at Worlds of Fun.

the other. I remember him trying to talk. He communicated by shaking his head "yes" or "no" in response to someone pointing to letters on a clipboard, spelling out words one letter at a time.

I knew Scott could process thoughts. One proof of this came from this exercise: Scott would sit on the edge of the bed with Grandma supporting him. He would put his feet on my legs as I sat on the floor. I would ask him a simple arithmetic problem, and he would tap out the answer on my legs with one of his feet!

During a visit one weekend, we took a shopping trip to a mall not too far from Rebound. It looked like Scott was starting to do much better. He tried on fifty pairs of sunglasses until he found just the right one. (It had Budweiser printed on it. I persuaded him to take his second choice.) Next, he chose a pair of tennis shoes by himself. He went to the pet shop twice to play with the dogs and even ate some candy I shouldn't have given him. The trip back to Rebound took just fifteen minutes. When Scott went inside and the nurses asked him where he had gone, he just shrugged his shoulders. He couldn't remember.

Our faith in God was our strength to help us through difficult times. I knew Scott could hear me before he could move. Before I left him at night, I would say the Lord's Prayer. After saying "Amen," he would breathe a deep, contented sigh. Many people who work for the same company as I, prayed for Scott, including some as far away as Canada, Germany, South Africa, and Brazil.

I visited Scott every weekend. We would go to church on Sunday. I remember in June of 1990 when I had to bodily lift him from the car to a wheelchair. I was so happy when he was able to walk up and kneel at the alter by himself.

One Monday morning during that same month, as I was driving back to Iowa from Kansas City, the sun was shining through the most beautiful white clouds. I heard a voice say, "He's going to be all right."

I thank God and all who have helped Scott on his road to recovery.

■　■　■　■　■

On The Rebound

I was surprised rehabilitation and therapy began almost immediately and did not take a backseat to the surgeries that accompanied my program at Rebound. I was so banged up it took fourteen operations before the damage done to my body was repaired as well as it could be.

In July 1990, Dr. Gregory Hummel lengthened my right leg. It was just after this surgery I started to remember things I could not previously recall. Other operations followed: October 1990—left arm lengthened; December 1990—right arm lengthened; February 1991—left hand brought out and fingers pinned out; June 1991—right hand brought out by rerouting a tendon from the bottom side of the wrist to the top side of the hand.

The most painful of all the operations—I wince at the thought even today—was the surgery on my hands. My hands and fingers had to be stretched out from the curled position they assumed during the coma. Nothing ever hurt as badly as that. My occupational therapist, Jane Cox, had to physically prestretch my fingers before surgery, and when she did, I cursed at her and cussed up a storm! I couldn't figure out why she was hurting me so much.

After I had surgery on my left hand, I relearned how to brush my teeth. It wasn't until after the surgery I could open my hand to put a toothbrush in it or turn it to reach my mouth.

Oddly, some of my indulgent attitude and behavior before the accident may have actually helped speed my recovery. Oleatta, the receptionist at Rebound, was single and a fox. I had the hots for her. I always perked up and was on my best behavior when I knew I'd have the chance to talk to her. I was at her desk as much as possible. Kathy Sloan, one of my nurses, was a gorgeous woman and a real inspiration for me to want to get better as fast as I could. I always thought on certain days she wore low-cut blouses, but that perception may have been more wish than reality. Oleatta and Kathy used to give me a little kiss for luck before each operation. In some way, that made me actually look forward to surgery.

I never thought I would have to learn to dress myself again. One of my major accomplishments was putting on my own socks without help. There I was, a grown man, understanding what to do but unable to do it because my brain wouldn't send the proper messages to my hands. It was a humbling experience. The cocky little boy was gone for good.

It was a personal milestone when I could get up from sitting or lying down and go to the bathroom alone. It signified what I hoped would be the first of many major accomplishments. It seems hard to believe something this simple could be so important, but it was. And although it was a long time ago, I've never forgotten how meaningful it was. I've reflected many times on how unexpectedly values can change your life.

For a long time, I had to read material in large print, designed for the visually impaired. Much of this was books designed for very young children—I hated having to read those kiddie books! But, like other parts of my body, the muscles in my eyes had been weakened and had to be built back up. I was very excited when I started to read the newspaper by myself. I still remember the date: January 25, 1992. I was so excited, I called Mom at home to tell her. This meant I would be all right on my own, if and when I returned to school.

One of the most important things that happened during my rehabilitation was realizing I could admit when I was wrong. Remember, I was used to calling all the shots. How ironic. Less than a year before the accident, I expected others to do things for me. Afterward, I needed people to do things for me. Although I was not inconsiderate before the accident, I learned at Rebound how to be more helpful to others. I found myself going out of my way to help people, especially those who were in worse shape than I was.

As I became more able to do things for myself physically, my emotions went through several phases. I went through a stage of anger. I was mad at the world in general. I was mad at myself for having reached the lowest point in my life. I threw what can only be called temper tantrums, lashing out at the people who were trying to help me. It infuriated me whenever someone at Rebound told me, "Be appropriate. Don't swear. Be kind to everybody." Thankfully, this period passed quickly.

Some of the doctors who examined me did not believe I'd ever be able to walk again. Others told me, "It is not going to be easy, but after what we've heard about you, if anyone can do it, you can." I never doubted for a moment, however, that I would walk again. The skepticism of the doctors who thought it was unlikely was offset by the encouragement of family, friends, and doctors who thought it might be possible.

There was much work to do in daily therapy sessions. I became focused on learning to walk again, and it became my number one personal goal at Rebound. It was very frustrating. Because I had walked all of my life before the accident, I knew how to walk. But my brain wouldn't send the signals to my legs to walk. At the very beginning of the therapy specifically designed to help me to walk again, one of the therapists said to me, "So you want to walk on your own? Well, get up and walk!"

I asked for help getting up from the chair I was in. Everyone, including me, was amazed when I took a small step forward with my left leg, alone. But when I went to move my right leg, *whomp!* They caught me before I fell flat on the floor. I was unable to use crutches to make learning how to walk easier. Because of my head injury, my arms were affected such that it was impossible for me to place crutches under them. It was either tough it out or not at all. But I never faltered in my belief that I would walk again.

Dance therapy may sound like a strange way to begin to teach someone to walk again, but it's really quite logical. Your dance "partner," a physical therapist, uses her arms to help you keep your balance, training those atrophied and unused muscles to feel what it's like to be working again. She helps keep you up in case you start to fall. And she decides how much is enough per session, so you're not fatigued and your muscles are not overly taxed. The rhythm of music also helps to act as a guide for simple movement. You might say it's the grandaddy of aerobic dancing.

I also used to practice just walking. It actually took a total of four people to get me walking when I took those first steps: One person had to hold up my butt, another held the rest of my body upright, a third shuffled my legs to create a walking rhythm, and a fourth person stood by in case any extra help was needed. Randy Leighton, a physical therapist, would put his arm around my waist for support or hold my hips up until the muscles were strong enough to support me without help. He also helped me walk up and down stairs without using a handrail. We started with just half a flight of steps at a time and progressed to four full flights. I went up and down those four flights of stairs every day for

Cindy helping me to walk steps.

a long time. The therapists cautioned me not to overdo it, but I've always been an overachiever and I pushed myself as hard as I could every time I exercised. Randy knew how important it was to me to be able to walk again, and he helped me a great deal.

I knew my legs (which had also been injured) would have to be strengthened considerably before I'd ever be able to walk again. Thanks to my sports background, I knew one way to do this. I worked with the therapists to develop a program of sit-ups. Once I started, I was not content to do sets of twenty-five, fifty, or even one hundred at a time. I usually did sets of three hundred. I got to the point where I could do well over a thousand per morning and afternoon session. Yes, it was hard work, but I could feel the muscles developing. I knew by sticking with it, I'd reach the day when I could say, "I can walk," much sooner.

It took over more than a year before I walked on my own again, but I'll never forget the date. It was on May 10, 1991, the high point of my rehabilitation.

All of the therapists and nurses at Rebound were masters of motivation. Cindy Reagan, my physical therapist, was the first therapist to teach me how to walk. I made a game of hiding and making her search for me. Betty Rugh, my night nurse, encouraged me to begin the sit-up program that strengthened my legs. I used to sleep from four o'clock in the afternoon until eight just so I could stay up and talk to her all night. She was my mother's age and gorgeous. (A lot of my old characteristics were coming through!) She was a real inspiration to me. She told me to get off the "pitty pot" and do something constructive like sit-ups.

Therapist Brad Jackson also helped me out. He was a big, strong black man whose sense of humor will stay with me forever. We always called each other "home boy." He is black and I am white, but we realized we both had the same creator. Kevin Birch, an on-call therapist, was like a big brother to me. He lived in one of the apartments at Rebound. I spent a lot of time in his apartment talking about anything and everything. Lee Harrison was my speech therapist. She was the first person to teach me to pronounce sounds and words again. Boy, was she patient! We would go through the alphabet and enunciate individual sounds, all simple things but very important to my recovery.

Kay Williams was my in-patient psychologist and also my second mother. She taught me how to have patience. She got me out of a lot of trouble with the nursing staff. I will always be greatly appreciative for all the troubles she helped get me out of and for helping me to understand.

Toward the end of my stay as an in-patient at Rebound, I got the feeling that the staff was ready for me to move ahead, to do more by myself. Creating this feeling of forward movement was the best thing they could have done for me. I was ready to take more control of my life. But I was not expecting a bigger change would happen—a change that helped to give me direction and purpose for the future.

Transition

TRANSITIONS

The following is the official list of qualifications from Rebound that must be met by patients advancing to the transitional phase of therapy. Note how most items are things people take for granted. It's somewhat unnerving to see them spelled out this way.

(Structured) Apartment Living Admission Criteria

1. Evidence of acquired brain injury (e.g., trauma, surgical, circulatory, anoxia)
2. Eighteen years of age or older
3. Cognitive level VII / VIII
4. Previously underwent some type of head injury rehabilitation therapy
5. Absence of communicable or contagious disease
6. Potential for further rehabilitation
7. Functional mobility
8. Functional communication
9. Ability to plan for future
10. Life Survival Skills
    a. Ability to plan daily activity
    b. Ability to plan and prepare all meals
    c. Ability to be independent in cleaning skills, laundry
    d. Ability to record information
    e. Ability to perform three-step problem solving

  f. Able to access community with assist from Rebound
   staff

11. Behavioral
  a. Ability to live with roommate
  b. Ability to negotiate
  c. Compliance with daily therapy schedule
  d. Has appropriate social skills
  e. Does not require supervision
  f. Understands rules and complies with them

NOTE: Rebound is now known as the Kansas City Rehabilitation Network. The name was changed after the HealthSouth Rehabilitation Corporation bought Rebound, Inc.

■ ■ ■ ■ ■

  The goal of the second part of Rebound's rehabilitation program is to help patients live independently. You are moved from living as an in-patient in a ward-like setting to living pretty much alone. One of the qualifications for advancing into this part is the ability to walk by yourself or to transfer yourself from a wheelchair without help. You live "on campus," but you have your own apartment, similar to a college dormitory. You're on your own, but there's a "safety net" close by if you need it. Once you've relearned the basics to get you through the day, you need to relearn how to live life as well as how to do life.

  Rather than being thrilled to move into my own apartment in April 1991, I was angry because the people at Rebound stopped doing things I could now do myself. No one waited on me anymore. I went through an anger stage during the early stages of in-patient rehabilitation, so I guess it wasn't unusual to have to pass through another one as I went through the early stages of transitional rehabilitation.

  As an in-patient, you learn simple movements and little things to make your mobility and mind-body coordination stronger. As a transitional patient, you learn more specific skills. I like to think of it as fine-tuning your life.

  It was during this transitional phase that I learned how to dress myself again. I remember the staff taking the shoelaces off my shoes and

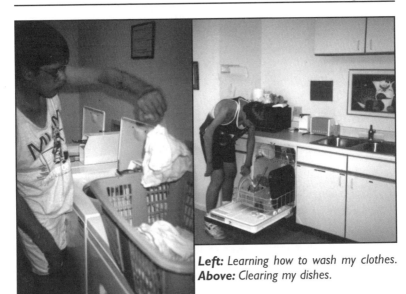

Left: Learning how to wash my clothes.
Above: Clearing my dishes.

attaching Velcro strips to "tie" the shoes, so I could get them on and off by myself. I learned how to wash my own clothes. I still ate meals in a cafeteria, but now it was up to me to clear my own dishes when I was finished. I joined other transitional patients in the cafeteria kitchen once a week to help prepare the food we ate, with the cooks giving us simple tasks to perform.

Before the accident I always thought of doing laundry, cooking, and cleaning as women's work. In transitional rehabilitation, I felt a sense of accomplishment when I was able to do it all for myself. These things became ordinary facts of life instead of tasks I once used to self-ishly manipulate others to do for me.

Dressing myself and going to the bathroom whenever I needed to without help from another person became daily pleasures for me. One of my most enjoyable pastimes was simply watching television and eating popcorn. Think about that for a minute—watching television and having a snack of your own choice. I suppose most people don't give watching television and having a snack a second thought. But suppose you were disabled so that:

You can't sit in a chair without help from someone.

You can't communicate that you want to watch TV or change channels.

You can't get up and move to do it yourself.

You can't adjust the volume to suit your comfort.

You can't prepare a snack because your hands and arms won't do what you want them to.

You can't eat a snack because your arm won't bend so your hand can reach your mouth.

Does that make it easier to understand how excited I was to be able to do something as simple as watch TV and eat popcorn?

Transitional life at Rebound was not without funny moments and fond memories. When you spend a lot of time with people, it's natural to develop friendships and bonds. My best friend at Rebound was a fellow patient named Kenny. He had fallen off the roof of a two-story house, injuring his head. Because of my own injuries, my speech was very poor then and it was difficult to understand what I was saying. Kenny had the same disability, but we could understand each other without any problem! It appeared to others we had a language of our own. We used to drive the nurses in the hospital crazy because we could conduct seemingly normal conversations and the nurses couldn't understand a word we were saying!

Kenny was very bright and a real inspiration to me. He had a positive outlook on everything. Being in a wheelchair didn't bother him a bit. He used to tease the nurses as much as I did. I was very happy when Kenny made it to the transitional phase. I think he was one of the few people there who really understood what I had been through as he and I shared some of the same physical problems.

Some patients in transition had roommates. I did not have one for a long time because of my preference for keeping the room temperature cool. Well, I called it cool; to many people, keeping the thermostat set at sixty degrees is downright cold. I took a lot of kidding about this. Kenny gave me a nickname that other patients picked up and used regularly. I didn't mind, because I thought it was funny and fitting. I was the Snowman. It was ironic, because "snow" also refers to drugs. Amazing irony or cosmic black humor? I don't want to guess.

As an in-patient, you're preoccupied with therapy and the "little things" that aren't so little any more. You have less time to think beyond yourself. In the transitional phase of life at Rebound, you have much more time to think, to reflect, to strengthen the part of your mind that considers abstract and philosophical ideas. This type of personal mental rehabilitation, relearning how to think by and for yourself, may be the most important part of the entire process.

One of the most significant things that happened to me during this part of my life came about as the result of a random event. I still needed a little help in putting on my coat. One cold day, I stopped a stranger and asked if he would help me put my coat on. He did, I thanked him, and he went on his way. He was just doing someone a simple favor. It was no big deal to him. But that small act made me realize that I could be accepted in the community by the world outside Rebound. It was a big deal to me.

This independent thinking probably helped me make the decision to stay in the transitional program at Rebound, although I had the opportunity to leave in August 1991. My decision was not based on fear or wanting others to do things for me. I wanted to stay to receive more therapy so I could be as healthy as possible, physically and mentally, when it came time for me to leave. And I wanted to stay to attend Longview College for a semester. Coach Shelling had always driven a famous quote into my head that Vince Lombardi made famous: "Be the best you can be."

Coming home from college. Randy Leighton and Kevin Birch watching.

Longview College in Lee Summit, Missouri, just south of Kansas City, had a special program in cooperation with Rebound designed for people with learning disabilities. Project Able concentrated on preparing you for the

Mary Ellen Jenison, director of Project Able.

end of your stay at Rebound. It was the last step before you walked back into a life of your own. Those of us who made it to Project Able were driven to class four days each week. Getting out and away from the familiar settings of Rebound and simply traveling back and forth to a college setting this way made me feel more a part of the outside world. I'll always be thankful to Mary Ellen Jenison, the director of Project Able. She is a remarkably patient, caring, and inspiring individual. She used to help me with my homework and always seemed to make time for me. I'll always be thankful for her help and guidance.

Along with traditional education came social learning. We attended group functions, such as outings to watch Kansas City Royals baseball games. That was an education in itself! Everyone likes to "people watch," but for myself and others at Rebound, this was a big dose of seeing how other people interact with each other on a grand scale, from ordinary conversation to heated differences of opinion, to finding their way around in a relatively unfamiliar setting.

And I thought it was just for fun!

The emphasis at Longview was on learning, and I welcomed it. No goofing off this time around. I wanted to make the most of this renewed educational opportunity. It was at Longview that I became aware that I would be able to continue learning at advanced levels. I had always been good in math and found I could understand beginning algebra without difficulty. I still couldn't read as well as I wanted to, but I never missed a class. I listened and memorized. I was a bit of a teacher's pet, an image I would have laughed at a couple of years earlier. I was a good example for other students, who helped me to take notes, since writing was still physically difficult for me.

I concentrated. I studied. I did it. I got straight A's.

I left Project Able feeling better about myself than I had in a very long time. I had relearned the routines of daily living, deepened my appreciation and understanding of relating to other people, and reaffirmed my ability to learn.

I left Rebound on April 10, 1992, exactly two and a half years after my accident. I had to be taken in. I walked out. I couldn't go to the bathroom by myself when I went there. I left knowing I could do almost anything for myself, by myself. I began the program as a humbled, crippled kid. I ended it as a modestly proud, healed young man.

But the biggest accomplishment I made in rehabilitation had nothing to do with any of this. It was the biggest thing that ever happened in my life. It provided an understanding of how and why my life had been such a roller coaster ride. And most importantly, it gave me a framework for both the immediate future and for the rest of my life. It was a discovery I never expected to make.

Reflections and a New Outlook

Do you believe in precognitive dreams? They're usually vivid dreams, easily remembered, and likely to be dismissed as "just a dream" by most people. I had one, and it did come true.

I dreamt about the car crash that put me into the coma.

It was a dramatic dream that has always stayed with me. I still remember the date I had it: April 20, 1989. Although I don't remember all of the details precisely, I do remember dreaming I was badly injured in a terrible automobile accident. I had the clear impression I had become an example for the world.

As frightening as it was, I brushed it off as only a bad dream, a drama created by my subconscious. I thought it couldn't be anything more than a morality play, a stupid dream with a Sunday school message to be a good little boy instead of a cool sports dude. I never for a moment thought this dream might be a warning or, at the very least, a plea from another part of me struggling to say, "Hey! You're headed for a crash!" either literally or figuratively.

Whether you interpret them as messages from God or from an inner part of yourself, such dreams are important and should not be disregarded. I believe this dream was such a message, and I'll always regret ignoring it.

But why should I have paid any attention to it? Before the accident, everything was now. The future was the date of the next football game. My personal future was waiting in some untouchable void. It was a future that could only be positive and bright.

Precognition was always a part of my life. Whether a natural sense lost for some unknown reason or a more direct message from God, I'm amazed at how many clues I'd had that something big was going to happen in my life soon after I got the clues.

A couple of weeks before the accident, for example, I asked Mom, "Do I have good hospitalization insurance?" She was surprised and wondered why I was asking. I spoke from the heart: "I don't think I'm going to live to be very old.... I don't think I'm going to see my twenty-first birthday." I had not been brooding; something inside seemed to prompt me at random to think like that.

Although I'm still alive and kicking and hope to be for a long time, I did not, in fact, see my twenty-first birthday. I turned twenty-one in the hospital in a pretty murky mental state.

I don't remember the day of the accident, but Mom remembers another unusual occurrence that morning. True to form, I was in a hurry, trying to avoid being late for work. I dashed out of the house, jumped into my car, revved it up, and pulled out of the driveway. Then, although I knew it might make me late, I pulled back into the driveway, jumped out, ran back into the house, gave Mom a big hug and a kiss, and said, "I love you, Mom. You're the greatest!"

Usually, I'd just hop in the car and go. But that day, something, some cue from deep inside, urged me to take the extra minute to run back inside to tell Mom I loved her. Whatever it was that led me to break my routine, I'm glad it happened. Those were the last words she heard me say for over a year. While I was in rehabilitation, I had time to think and to ask myself serious questions. When all you can do is lie in bed for long periods of time, you have no choice but to think. Although I was determined to walk again and was motivated enough to flirt, the extent of my injuries and the sense of loss I felt combined at times to make me think about the unthinkable: suicide.

There were times when I was in the hospital I really wanted to die. I did not realize how precious life is. I relived my sports victories over and over again in my mind, and I became depressed when I realized that it would never be that way again. My old way of life—the parties, drugs, sports, and women—was ingrained. My desire for that life did not end quickly. When physical gratification is reinforced over and over, it becomes addictive—very much like using drugs.

The friendships I started to develop with other Rebound patients became important to me. I was touched every day by the caring of Rebound staff members who wanted to help me grow stronger. I was—perhaps for the first time—learning the value of the important things in life. I knew I would go to hell if I killed myself. I had never been motivated by fear before, but things were different now. I accepted the fact I wasn't such a hotshot less reluctantly than I would have earlier in my life. It's not difficult to do when you realize your body is literally bent out of shape.

But I could not ignore the support and love of my family, especially my mother. I was very much aware of what killing myself would do to them. None of the people closest to me ever lost faith. No one believed I would not come out of the coma. I knew if I killed myself, these people would not only be deeply hurt but would feel they had failed in some way. I could never accept failure for myself, so how could I do something that would cause those who loved me to feel they had failed?

It was, and is, the easy way out. If you look into the mirror, you will always find the answers to your problems staring right back at you. One of the things I thought about at Rebound was knowing how it felt to be disabled. In these days of being politically correct, let's use the right word: disabled not challenged. Challenges can be met. The career I wanted for myself had been wiped out. I was disabled. At times, I was sad and angry thinking about it. But I managed to accept my situation by consistently thinking, "How do I cope with this? What do I need to do to keep going?"

Others can empathize all they want in trying to imagine what it feels like to be disabled. But unless it happens to you, you can never fully understand it. I gained a real appreciation of those who can't do for themselves, because for a while I was one of them.

You never think to yourself, "So this is what it's like." Your attitude gradually changes until, for example, seeing someone in a wheelchair evokes no reaction whatsoever. That person is just part of the picture and not necessarily a person who needs a special accommodation.

One victory I took great pride in during rehabilitation was learning to be left-handed. My right hand was injured so much that I cannot use my fingers normally. My left hand, although it had been injured too, was more flexible. So on the recommendation of doctors, I became left-handed.

The problem was that my mind was right-handed. I had lived twenty years as a right-handed person. It seemed unnatural to do things with my left hand. Many, many times I started to do something with my right hand and then I would remember, "Oh, yeah, I gotta do this with my other hand." Frustrating, aggravating, sometimes comical, I slowly learned to make my left hand the dominant one. Today, whenever someone who doesn't know how this came to be kids me about being left-handed, I like to zap them back by saying, "Only left-handed people are in their right mind!"

Spend an hour sometime trying to use the hand you don't usually use. Forget writing—just try dressing yourself, tying your shoes, combing your hair, and even eating with the other hand. You'll gain an understanding of this problem very quickly and, in doing so, personally share one of the challenges I faced.

■ ■ ■ ■ ■

When I began learning again how to walk up and down stairs without using a handrail, I realized again how much of life we take for granted. At first I thought, "This must sound really stupid to most people." But I remembered how I used to go up and down the bleachers at different sporting events in high school. Bleachers don't have handrails except on the outside supports. If you have trouble moving or walking normally, lack of physical support can be both frightening and dangerous to you and to others. I felt a great sense of accomplishment when I was able to walk up and down steps without needing a handrail. It was as if I had regained a part of my former life—certainly a reason for at least a small celebration. When I was "officially" out of rehab and back home, one of the most unexpected and unusual situations I encountered was seeing my friends for the first time in many months. Brad Hansen, a football player and all-sports star athlete from my high

Standing in front of my trophy case holding the ball I hit a grand slam home run with against Missouri Valley.

school's arch rival Missouri Valley High school, even came to visit me. We had been extremely competitive, so I was surprised when he said to me, "If anyone could have come back, you could." His respect for me had extended beyond the playing field.

Many friends had come to see me right after the accident before I left the hospital in Omaha when I was in very bad shape. Most were shocked when they first saw me walking and talking. I was somewhat uncomfortable at this type of reception, but I knew their reactions were just part of the changes accompanying what I could rightfully call a rebirth, a new life. Some friends were afraid to approach me, probably because they didn't know what to expect. Some would come close and ask, "Do you remember me?"

This made me angry. I wanted to shout back at them, "Why wouldn't I remember you?" I realized, however, they knew I had sustained head injuries, undergone more than two years of therapy, and had no real news about me for months. I assume some must have felt bad because they had not visited me after I left the hospital in Omaha. I understood this—they had their own lives to live. And I was three hours away in Missouri. Friends are not always as close as family and that's okay.

One thing that does bother me is my lack of recollection for certain events. It always hurts me when someone asks, "Do you remember when…?" about a particular event or shared time in the past, and I have to answer, "No, I'm sorry, I don't remember."

■　■　■　■　■

Near the end of my stay at Rebound, I felt very good about myself and all of my personal accomplishments. This was not an attitude of conceit, but rather was part of the realization this part of my life was nearing an end. It was then I began to realize the things important to me before the accident were no longer important. I realized, for example, that I had come to really enjoy learning.

And yet, these changes did not seem dramatic to me. They were natural, almost logical results of rehabilitation and having had time to think. I discovered things about myself I never expected to find.

Discovery

As a youngster growing up in Iowa, my religious life was probably like that of many other kids. I went to Sunday school and attended church with my family. When you're a kid, you do it because it's expected of you and because you really have no choice.

When I became a teenager, my beliefs stayed the same but grew less intense and not as important. It wasn't "cool" to be active in religious activities. Mom tried to maintain my involvement with our faith but respected my right to make my own decisions. Unfortunately, at that time, faith was no match for sports, drugs, and sex. Any church services or functions I attended were done more for the sake of appearance than anything else.

It may sound contradictory, but although I was very self-centered before the accident that put me into the coma, I've always supported the so-called underdogs in life. In particular, I remember a short, black student in high school. He received a fair amount of taunting and teasing from other students on a regular basis. Keep in mind, there weren't many black students in small, rural Iowa high schools at the time. I didn't know him personally, and I didn't know whether or not there was any racial prejudice involved in his being teased, but it annoyed me. One day, as several students were harassing him, I stepped in and said, "Anyone who wants to hassle him has to deal with me first." Everyone backed off.

I wasn't trying to impress anyone. I just felt he was being treated unfairly, and I wanted to straighten the situation out.

At Rebound, I began to appreciate the fact that, in spite of my problems, there were others who were in worse condition than I was. I did not especially pity them, but I felt for them. I went out of my way to help them if they needed and wanted it. I helped others more often than I realized at the time. Without knowing it, I was learning to enjoy being in service to others, and I received a great deal of satisfaction from it.

Enter the Junk Food Man, also known as Bob Zerr. He was the spiritual counselor at Rebound, and although Bob wasn't the chaplain, he did a chaplain's service, helping to meet the religious needs of all the patients there. He took us to the chapel, conducted services himself once in awhile, and could rightfully be called Rebound's religious ombudsman.

Bob had a wonderful personality. He smiled a lot and was very reassuring to everyone. Although he never passed up an opportunity to try to persuade you to attend services or visit the chapel, he never leaned on you. His suggestions to beef up your spiritual life were never threatening or heavy-handed.

I liked Bob a lot—at first because he supplied me with snacks I wasn't supposed to have. That's how he got the nickname Junk Food Man. I'm sure Rebound would not have been happy to learn how much candy and sweet stuff he provided for me.

Bob was always asking me to go to the chapel. And I always said no. I had no interest in hearing someone preach.

Then one day, I asked Bob to take me to the chapel.

He laughed, thinking I was making a joke of some kind. But I wasn't. Make no mistake: I did not have some kind of dramatic revelation, some blinding flash of realization that said I must be born again. It wasn't a desperate move, a quick decision. It was simply the right thing to do.

I had nowhere else to go but up. I didn't like the position I was in and was willing to do anything to get out of it. I was still determined to walk and to lead a normal life again someday, but I was tired. I knew it was God who had pushed away my thoughts of suicide. And I had a feeling I had been spared from death in both accidents for a reason other than extreme luck.

Bob was delighted. He took me to the chapel where he read from the Bible. I let myself open up and felt a great sense of calm and satisfaction. Realizing I was still recuperating and in therapy, Bob frequently asked me, "Do you want to stop now?" But I felt so good, I answered, "No," every time. We read for three and a half hours.

I went to the chapel every chance I could after that. I never grew tired of hearing someone read from the Bible and later of reading it myself. I found answers to questions I had thought about many times at Rebound. I understood what had happened to me and why. I discovered that being born again means being figuratively reborn for yourself, as well as for God.

Two things became clear soon after I started to go to the chapel regularly. I knew God had spared my life in the first car crash because he was trying to teach me a lesson, to give me a second chance. I am sure He was warning me. It was a stiff warning, but at the time, it was the only type of language I understood...and I still didn't listen! I know He's forgiven me, but I still have moments from time to time when I feel deep regret for not listening earlier.

It also became clear God had a purpose for me going through what I did. I wasn't sure at the time what it was, but today I am: God saved me so I could help others.

The enjoyment of helping others at Rebound while being severely challenged myself laid the groundwork to make my decision to rediscover God more natural and easy. I went from virtually no religion to too much religion. I wanted to spread the word to everybody. I became a pest. Thanks to Bob's guidance and the patience I learned as a result of my extended recuperation, I learned to keep my passion for preaching under control.

I still get so excited sometimes I have to remind myself God speaks to each person only at the speed at which they can hear. I continue to strive for balance today.

Before my second accident, I went to church occasionally just to see my friends and please my mother. Now I go every Sunday for the right reasons: to worship God and to thank Him for all He has done for me. I know God guided the hands of all the doctors who operated on me and gave me the strength to pull through fourteen surgeries. If I ever start feeling down, all I have to do is to watch some of the videotape made of me just before I began rehabilitation. I look terrible and fairly hopeless. Seeing it reminds me how powerful the Lord is. I wouldn't be anywhere without Him.

Old habits really do die hard. From time to time, I have flashes of the "old" Scott trying to come through, to return to the lifestyle that almost destroyed me. But the "new" Scott wants to leave him dead and buried. I hate the devil with a passion.

One of the things I've done to mark the transition from my druggie days to now is to change my name. I was Scott Krumwiede; now I'm Scott McPhillips. McPhillips is my father's name. He died when I was quite young. Everyone in my family says he was strong-willed and I look and act like him. Changing my name signifies a new start, as well as going back to my roots. And getting back to your roots means getting back to God.

And besides, I like the nickname "Mac."

■ ■ ■ ■ ■

For the longest time, I wondered why I had to go through everything I did as a result of the second car crash. I know now it was not a punishment. It was a random act, caused by my stupidity. God felt bad about it, too. He doesn't want to see us hurt ourselves. Yes, God has control over everything. But he gave us free will and keeps His hands off when we make a decision that results in pain. If he didn't, it wouldn't really be free will. Thankfully, His love and healing power gives us the way to correct our mistakes.

And for some of us who need it, He gives a second chance at life, too.

■ ■ ■ ■ ■

I've kept a personal journal for a long time. I started it during rehabilitation, having other people, especially my mother, write down my thoughts for me. In looking over the notes I made at the beginning of 1992, I'm reminded of the determination that has always been such a strong part of my life. I still feel today the way I did then when I wrote, "I believe deep in my heart that I can become whatever I really set my mind to. I can accomplish anything."

I want to coach someday. As a matter of fact, I want to coach a state championship. This isn't a way of trying to recapture past personal glories. Thanks to the Lord, I know I'm on a mission to teach all I know to youths so they will not have any of the pitfalls I had.

Coaching will have to have to wait for a little while, though. Right now, I want to tell my story to as many people as possible. That's why I wrote this book. That's why I speak to groups whenever I can.

The message is simple: Don't do drugs.

But it's getting harder and harder to get the message across. "Just say no" is a great idea but it's too simplistic. Nothing beats experience, and Lord knows, I've had that! No one should have to go through what I did.

I don't want to preach. I want to tell my story. People listen to stories and can learn from them. Hellfire, brimstone, and damnation only work on people who are already frightened. I hope if young people can identify with me, they might vicariously share even a little of my experience and get the message. It's a lot easier to learn from seeing someone else burn their fingers on a hot stove than to do it yourself.

It makes me feel really good when I know people hear what I'm saying. I spoke to a group of head-injured patients and their families at St. Joseph's Hospital in Omaha while I was completing my rehabilitation. I could see hope in their eyes when I told them I had been in worse condition than they were then. I was thrilled to be an inspiration to them.

Following some high school presentations, I've had one or two students come up to talk with me following my speech. I remember one girl who was crying as she approached. I said to her, "Hey, stop crying. This isn't a sad occasion. This is a happy occasion. I can talk and walk, and you heard what I said." She was sorry for what I had gone through and it moved her deeply. I knew my message was indeed being heard.

I spend a lot of time now talking to people everywhere about God and his message. The thank you notes and letters I've received are some of my greatest rewards. I spoke at Beveridge Junior High School and Benson High school in Omaha, Nebraska, and got a very special letter. I was told some of the Benson students had been moved to tears. In addition, the following thoughts were expressed:

> Your message is very personal and very painful. The issue of drunk driving or driving under the influence of any drugs is current and sometimes tragic. Because your message is so personal, it really does have power. The format of starting with the "healthy" video and having your mother talk while the rehabilitation film plays silently in the background is very effective. Young people tend to forget that their actions do affect other people. When you follow this and start talking about the emotional pain (losing your friend and your life as you knew it), and the physical pain, it becomes phenomenally powerful. I believe you are right Scott. You have had 2 strikes but you're not going to strike out. You are going to the TOP! Thank you so much.

Another note had these encouraging thoughts:

> I just wanted to let you know that I enjoyed visiting with you on Saturday. It was a most interesting story that you have to tell, as for the difficulties and adjustments that you had to adjust to. You are truly an amazing young man to have the positive attitude you do. Keep up the good attitude and the Lord will *guide* you.

> I participated in a mini-course day at the Logan-Magnolia Community School District in Logan, Iowa, which was very well received; I've been invited to participate in the next one. I've spoken to young people at shopping malls, where on more than one occasion, I've been told that people have rediscovered their relationship with God after hearing my story. This is what it takes for me to feel good about my life now. What a contrast with how I used to try to make myself feel good.

■ ■ ■ ■ ■

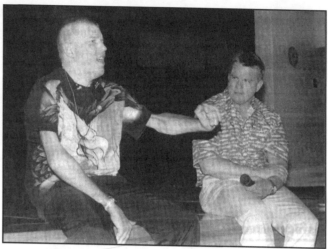

Coach Gaylord Schelling and I talking to the Atlantic kids.

Another high point for me is a newspaper article about me and my high school coach—and friend—Gaylord Schelling. The article by Colleen Mullen of the Atlantic *News-Telegraph* (Iowa) (April 4, 1997) details my past life and the accident, and how this can make students think about what the consequences may be of abusing alcohol and drugs.

...But they also see "his [Scott's] will to live, his will to win. He refused to die at that time [of the accident]," Schelling added. "...Often times it's easy for someone to give up. People have to see in life, if you have a will, you can make it."

Some people may feel sorry for what happened to him, but Scott does not feel sorry for himself. He believes it is not too late to influence others, make a difference in others' lives, and live an enriched, full life in the eyes of God.

...Things people take for granted each day, was something Scott was challenged with. But he didn't give up. Schelling can vouch for that.

"Right now, he's a good example to others," he said.

He's someone who values each breath he takes, each step he is able to walk.

Each day he has to face what happened on that grim day.

Each day he works to make amends with God, and asks for his forgiveness.

Gaylord Schelling always kept up with my rehabilitation and recovery, even after he left Tri-Center High School to take a coaching job in Atlantic, Iowa. I was honored when he asked me to talk to his team the night of their eighth game, following seven straight losses, in October 1991. I was a little apprehensive at the thought of speaking for my former coach in a setting that would bring together the good times that had been so important to me and the reality that I had caused my own dreams to be shattered.

I wrote the speech without much trouble. Because of my injuries, I could not speak well enough then to deliver the talk. Even today, sometimes it's physically difficult for me to speak. I asked Bryan White to deliver my speech. Bryan was a high school classmate I always thought of as a real goody-two-shoes. Today, he's one of my closest friends.

This is what I wrote and what Bryan said:

Coach Schelling has asked me to say a few words to you.

What do I think it takes to win? I strongly believe it takes hard work and heart in wanting something more than you have ever wanted something before.

Say you are behind in the fourth quarter—somehow, some way, you will find a way to win. I was never supposed to walk but I would not believe that. Don't you believe it when people say you are not supposed to win. Find a way to win, somehow, some way.

If you have any belief in Coach Schelling, you will give the game your all. You have to give the game your all. I did not realize how lucky I was until I lost it; now I'm having to give it my all just to try to be normal.

Remember, you have to believe in yourself and others will learn to believe in you. If you believe you are defeated, you are defeated. So believe you are a winner and come back after the game a winner. Now, go fight, and do it for yourself. The one you really have to please is yourself.

My biggest words of wisdom are the ones I live by every day: persistence overcomes resistance. That's how I've come as far as I have. My doctor said I would never walk, but I would not believe him. It all comes down to what you believe in your heart. If you believe you are always going to come out a winner, you will win. It all comes from the heart.

I knew many people who were more talented than I was, but I would not accept defeat at their hands. I would give anything to be able to do it all over again, but now you have to do it for me.

I am with you all the way.

Coach Schelling's team beat Glenwood 33–32 that day—Atlantic's only win of the season.

■　■　■　■　■

And I am with *you* all the way, too. Thank you for reading my story. May God bless you.

Scott McPhillips From the Eyes of Others

FROM SCOTT'S MOM

Life is full of good times and challenges. God never gives us more than we can handle, but raising Scott made me wonder more than once!

Scott was a very strong willed little boy who always wanted to be as big as his older brother. He played very hard and always strived to be the best.

His accomplishments in sports brought much happiness to me. All the way from PeeWee baseball to the Iowa State Tournament, I loved to sit behind the fence and watch him pitch. To watch him outjump 6'5" basketball players or catch the winning touchdown in football made me proud to be known as "Scott's mom." But, watching Scott overcome the injuries and trauma of his head injury by far exceeded any previous mother to son admiration.

When Scott came home from Rebound, April 10, 1992, exactly 2½ years after his accident, I took him to Immanuel Hospital for additional therapy. When tested for speech accuracy, he had an 11% intelligible factor. They taped a conversation and another therapist wrote down what was understandable.

When Scott started Iowa Western Community College in the fall of 1992, he was still at the same intelligible factor. They gave him a private room, since no one could share a room at 60 degrees. Scott's temperature control in his brain was damaged and he was always hot. The only way we could ride in comfort was if he wore shorts and a tank top and I wore a sweatshirt and winter coat. Of course when we stopped anywhere, accusing eyes said, "You don't even put a coat on this disabled kid?"

Another reason for staying alone was sleep patterns. Sometimes he would be up most of the night with sleeplessness. Studying took total concentration. We got tapes from the visually impaired on the subjects he took. I'll never forget one class we couldn't get tapes for. I worried over what we could do. They said it would take four months to tape and by that time the class would be over. One night coming home from work while driving, I talked to God. While asking God what can I do, a voice said to me "Tape it yourself." How easy answers can be sometimes. The only request Scott made was that someone else do the taping since he heard mom's voice so much.

The college let us remodel his dorm key. A rod was welded onto the key and a hole through the rod and put on a necklace to go around his neck. His hands were not able to get keys out of his pocket.

Life became a new ritual. Scott had a refrigerator in his dorm room in which he kept his doughnuts and milk for breakfast and snacks for lunch. I got off work at 3:30 p.m., picked up Scott to go out for dinner, talked over the goodness and problems of the day, helped with any homework left to do, and anything else that needed to be done. His hands were good enough to take care of his body needs, but not to do everything that needed to be done (clean room, washing clothes—woman's stuff). I wanted to make his stay at college as easy as possible. Scott could have gone to the college cafeteria to eat, but that was across campus. I was afraid he would be too tired after a long day and would go hungry rather than go to the cafeteria. Scott's eating habits were still not the best at this time. Due to the head injury when trying to eat, his hands would shake and the food would fall off the fork before getting to his mouth.

Most of the kids at IWCC were really helpful and kind—being 18 years old, taking the patience and time to listen to a young man with an 11% intelligible factor who walked with an unsteady gait. After 3 months at IWCC, Scott's intelligible factor increased dramatically because he talked so much and was trying harder than ever to make himself understood. With all those pretty girls around, he wanted them to know what he was saying. Same old charmer Scott.

There was always the worry during the winter months—icy sidewalks—but mostly his inability to feel cold. One day when it was -60 degrees wind chill factor, he walked all the way across campus with just a t-shirt and sweatpants on. He very seldom wore a coat as it was too hard to get on, he got too hot when he got into a building, and it was too hard to carry when he took it off.

Scott really enjoyed his stay at Iowa Western. He greatly advanced both physically and spiritually. I have to believe he was a bit favored by most. He had many who helped him. At the top of the list was Mike Wulbecker who helped him physically in the weight room, emotionally to deal with everyday situations, and to continue his spiritual walk with God. He was as a father to Scott, listening, disciplining as necessary, and being the friend he needed. David Hufford helped with his drinking problem, taking him to AA, and became a good friend. Being Scott, not afraid to talk to anyone, the Dean of IWCC, Robert Franzese, did not escape Scott on a daily basis.

As Scott states, "I have to mention the woman who put up with a lot of my crap, Jeanne Snyder. Jeanne helped me with reading and writing and my temper. I'm sure I tried her patience as much as she tried mine. I loved her and she appreciated and loved me. She has done extensive study on head injuries since I've left and she says it really helped her understand why I was the way I was. Iowa Western was just the place I needed to be. The people were very caring and loving. I have been back since I graduated, and it is still a great school. They have no one like I was—lucky for them."

Another challenge—Scott wanted to start driving again. Trying to give Scott a new outlook on life, we looked for and bought a new car in July 1993. Little did I know when we bought this red 1993 Pontiac Sunbird with black interior, fancy rim wheels, great radio system, cassette player, spoiler, etc. that he would actually get a license soon. It was like a catalyst and in November 1993 I finally gave in and said he could take the test for a permit to learn to drive. Without even reading or preparing for the driver's test, he passed with flying colors. The license bureau read the questions and answers for him and he responded with the answer. At this point it was still difficult to read. The muscles in his eyes were better, but still not focusing right to read.

Now we had a new challenge. At least Scott didn't want to drive on icy roads, so there was a little reprieve. In May 1994, he wanted to take the driving test to get his license. I wanted him to wait. When he was driving out of town one night, I told him to slow down, that he was going too fast. He said he wasn't, that the speed limit was 40 MPH. I said 35. He said if I'm right will you let me try for my license. I said yes because I knew I was right. I don't know when they changed the limit, but an agreement is an agreement.

The first time he failed and the examiner said she could have passed him, but she wanted him to have more driving practice. She felt he would not stay on the back roads for awhile, but would drive right in downtown Omaha immediately. I said, "Thank you." She had good perception. We drove and drove for a week and went back for retesting. They drove for a half hour during rush hour traffic on the main streets. He came back in with the biggest grin and she said he had points to spare. Lost the red car with less than 12,000 miles on it. Those wheels never stop now, 90,000 and continuing. Independence has never meant so much to Scott as well as to mom.

Today, Scott and I love to talk to school children, or anyone that will listen. The dead silence and respect that is shown, indeed reflects that our message is being heard. "Drugs are a lie, Jesus is the truth." Starting with a healthy video, highlights of a sports jock, to the Rebound video, the virtually hopeless young man through his next 26 months of recovery, played in silence while we talk. I'll always wish I would have had more "tough love" while Scott was growing up and maybe we could have eliminated some of the pitfalls. We truly hope that people can learn for us instead of going through the trials and tribulations we have had to face.

I have a real admiration for my son, the challenges he has faced, and his love and commitment to God. He never ceased to amaze me with the play to win the game, but now the greatest game of all, "The Game of Life." I am honored to be know as "Scott's mom."

FROM DAVID HUFFORD

I first met Scott McPhillips when he was a student at Iowa Western Community College sometime in 1993, and have remained his friend until this day. He was never a student of mine, but never has a person been more a student of mine. My first impression of Scott—I blush to admit it—was being not a little frightened of him. I did not know Scott as he was, as I had heard he was. I had heard he had been a fine student of great promise, and an excellent, a great, athlete. I had heard he had gone away to college, and had been in a terrible accident. That was all I knew. I had no particular expectations. And since Scott had never been in any of my classes, I had had no occasion to talk to him.

I probably would not have talked to him. Scott presented a rather fearful aspect. It was not just the fact that some miracle of modern medicine had pieced together the man who I saw, but that Scott was also frightening of aspect, with a loud, but unsteady voice, and an intense demeanor.

When at last I chanced to meet him—he had come to the English Department Office to see someone else—he stopped to talk to me. I was uncertain how to proceed—Scott's enunciation becomes clear enough when you are familiar with it—but I suddenly felt a need to communicate. And I as Communication teacher, was uncertain how to proceed. The opening came on two or three points of truth: we both insisted on the truth—hard line truth. We both insisted on fearlessly stating and expounding our religious convictions and spiritual insights, and we both had some kind of problem with alcohol. I am an alcoholic. Scott needed to talk to someone about things which also apparently included just needing to speak freely and truthfully, to talk about his deepening belief, and to talk about problems of his medical and physical condition, his past, his wreck, his purportedly previous drinking that had led to his personal disaster.

All these things he told me in painfully slow and broken sentences. When he stopped at some point, I was immediately all over him: I recall my first sentence to a man who had frightfully suffered more than most of us will know: "Clean the wax out of your ears."

What I believe I was hearing at that point is what admitted and recovering alcoholics refer to as *denial*. Scott had been through much in his physical and mental recovery, but there was still much churning around in him of an emotional and spiritual nature.

Later it would come out always in terms of how much Jesus Christ had done for him, the power of which Scott was possessed to do the will of God, as of one powerfully converted by the most astonishing of circumstances; for that is actually what the situation was. But I felt there were issues which Scott was not dealing with, sometimes admitting, but not totally acknowledging.

But to tell such a person to clean the wax out of his ears was a harsh beginning. But it got his attention—not because I was out to get his attention, but that I had one thing to offer him: I had suffered different things but for the same reason: the bottle. And I had also done damage while drunk. And I had to admit not my power but my powerlessness, and turn my will and life over to God. I drank not because of some madman's insane desire for alcohol, but why all of us do: that one drink will trigger an obsession that will not let us stop. And we drink to fill some interior black hole that nothing will fill.

Scott was trying to fill the black hole with the right stuff without going through the process of getting back out of where he had gotten. Religion, positive thinking, education, hard work—all are fine things, but what some of us need is an inside job.

Scott was arrested by my candor, and thereafter we could always talk openly about everything. (Eventually this entailed going to AA meetings.) My office became a more exciting place of dialogue than most classrooms. We could seek the truth in utter disagreement while deeply respecting the spoken spirituality we were both capable of stating. Nevertheless it was not until after Scott could say "I killed a man," and "I drove after I lined up ten shots of Jack Daniels," that the blockade was cleared.

Scott began to pull away from organized recovery groups, for his spiritual bent was more in the direction of the open declaration of what Jesus Christ had done for him. But I think the exchange of his ideas with others in recovery was valuable for all of them.

It is clear that Scott has a message that is born of suffering and the positive lessons that one can turn such an experience into. Scott goes many directions: I will try to get him to keep it simple, as in Christ's words. "Fear not; only believe." Both of us are similar in belief: both deriving from Lutheranism, both spiritual mavericks.

Through our various sufferings, we learn to love, to seek justice, and to forgive. It would be wrong to suggest that Scott and I have been these great spiritual geniuses: we are buddies who became friends. We have talked as much about women and sex as about God and recovery. We are men.

But Scott has helped me become more the kind of man I also need to be: one more like him: more willing to witness, more willing to speak the nearest good thing and to do the first best thing. Scott has taught me to be unafraid to speak and do my convictions as fearlessly as he does.

FROM DEAN ROBERT FRANZESE

I first met Scott in the fall term of 1992. This was the first time that I would ever set eyes on Scott. I must admit, I was startled by his condition, which I knew nothing about at that time. Scott walked very slowly and cautiously, and his speech was nearly unintelligible for me. I first encountered Scott as he was walking into a psychology course taught by Terry Miller. Scott approached Terry and proceeded to attempt to explain to him his needs, which quickly became apparent. Scott was going to need special attention and services, which the College has provided to its students throughout its history. During that first encounter with Mr. Miller and me, Scott told us of his automobile accident that was responsible for his disabilities. It was a very sad story, and it was extremely difficult to understand Scott. His speech was slurred, and the words spoken were indistinguishable from one another.

To state that Scott was a "unique" individual would be a major understatement. He continued for at least a full semester to walk very slowly, and to speak in an unclear manner. But by the spring term, Scott had begun to walk with more confidence, and his speech improved markedly, although he was still difficult to understand. His turnaround appeared to have a lot to do with Mike Wulbecker, who at that time was the athletic director and professor of physical education. Mr. Wulbecker took Scott under his wings, and worked with him daily, on his speech and on his physical condition. As a result, Scott became stronger and more confident. He also began to become more appreciated by his student peers. With his increasing self confidence, Scott's grades also improved, and Scott made the great strides needed to proceed down the path toward graduation.

Scott graduating from Iowa Western Community College, August 1, 1994.

As Scott assimilated more into Iowa Western, he became quite the admirer of the coed population (something tells me that this had always been an interest of Scott's). He was seen frequently with women—even if they did not invite him into their conversations or where they were seated. But Scott was making progress with every day: he spoke more clearly, and carried himself with pride and positive demeanor. In one year, Scott became a "new man," and during this period, this formerly perplexed young man found faith, again through the efforts of Mike Wulbecker.

For me, the defining point in my experience with Scott was when he graduated from Iowa Western during the summer of 1994. To see him walk across the stage and receive his degree was a highlight of my 23 years with the college. In all respects, Scott has changed for the better, and he continues to have goals and to grow as a man with a bright future.

FROM TODD HARRISON

I met Scott several years ago. I remember how he was so willing to talk to whoever would listen. Very shortly after that first meeting, Scott was a student in Public Speaking class. I thought to myself, Will Scott get along in this class with other students? Will he be able to get his point across in the assigned speeches? I saw Scott, in the middle of winter, walking up College Road with no coat or hat on. I had to approach him the next day to ask "why?" He simply told me he didn't need a coat or hat, and that was that. During the semester and years afterward I learned a lot about Scott. His aspirations, his beliefs, and his determination. He inspired so many people, because Scott is not a quitter.

He did well in Public Speaking, always volunteered to be first to speak, which made the other students happy. He fulfilled Speech assignments like a champ. Other students got to know Scott. They respected him and listened to his message about not giving up. I think over the years Scott and I became friends. At least, I hope so, because he has been an inspiration to me.

On the Rebound

Written by Bill Henjum for Scott McPhillips

Bill: You've probably read about someone who has been drunk in a car accident where a life has been lost. You've probably read about someone who's been in a coma for months. You've probably read about someone who's had to blink once for "yes" and twice for "no."

Scott: You've probably read about someone like me.

I will go back to the time when I was known as Scott Krumwiede. He was a very wild little boy. He played very hard and he's paid very hard. I'd like to share a little about me today.

In high school I was one cocky little boy. I was at the top of the world.

Bill: Scott was at the top of the world. He was an all-state athlete in football, basketball, and baseball, and had a reasonable chance of becoming a professional athlete. I'll tell you why.

In 1985 and 1986, he helped his team, the Tri-Center Trojans from Neola, Iowa, to second place finishes, runner-ups, in the state basketball and baseball tournaments, and Scott's team also made the state football play-offs.

In one football game, he caught a 65-yard reception for a touchdown and ran 55 yards for another to win the game against Griswold, 26–25. As a senior on the basketball team, he averaged 26 points and 12 rebounds a game. However....

Scott: I do not remember the greatest accomplishment of my sports career.

Bill: Scott and the Trojans were the Iowa state baseball champions in 1987.

Scott: They tell me I pitched a pretty good game. The first time at bat, I hit a home run.

Bill: For his pitching and hitting, he was named the Most Valuable Player for the tournament.

Scott: I'm sure you can understand how much it bothers me that I can't remember events going back to 1986. I can't even remember being the MVP of the state championship.

Bill: In the fall of 1987, this cocky little boy was off to Simpson College in Indianola, Iowa. He went there because he could play ball.

Scott: I went there to have fun, but it was the wrong kind of fun, and I'll tell you why in a moment.

Bill: As a freshman, Scott started on the varsity football team at free safety. He was known as the maniac.

Scott: On a Wednesday night after the fifth football game, my friend and I were out.

Bill: Boozing it up after a trip to Des Moines in his brother's new, black Eurosport.

Scott: Having what we thought was fun. And wham.

Bill: No one knows what happened exactly, but the car ended up against a guardrail. They told him that he wasn't driving.

Scott: All I can remember from that wreck is running down the railroad tracks and falling in the cinders with a broken bone sticking out of my arm.

Bill: The cops caught him, and he was helicoptered to the hospital in Des Moines.

Scott: Lucky or not, the cops never took a blood sample, but the hospital sample was .04 (dead drunk). God was trying to teach me a lesson that time, but I didn't learn, true to form.

Bill: It was a struggle to come back after the accident, but he made the varsity baseball team as a pitcher. It was tough to hit because of his broken arm, but he could still pitch.

Scott: And, boy, they wanted me to pitch. Anyone with a 94-mile-per-hour fast ball can blow them away.

Bill: That spring, while throwing batting practice, a line-drive hit right back at him; fractured his right eye socket.

Scott: Which ended my spring training trip to Florida. And boy, did I want to see those bikinis.

Then on October 10th, 1989, my body and my whole world were shattered. The car I was driving collided head-on into an oncoming vehicle, driven by my friend and my brother's best friend.

Bill: It happened on a gravel road at the crest of a hill. He was coming home from a bar, drunk, which was nothing new. As a matter of fact, his blood alcohol was .014 five hours after the wreck, which means he had been dead drunk.

Scott: And my friend—my brother's best friend—was killed. Lucky or not, I lived. I am very thankful now. The message came through that time, loud and clear.

Bill: It took ten hours of surgery to put his body back together again and save his life.

Scott: I never want anyone here to experience how it feels to know someone has died because of your stupidity. Whenever I think about it, which is often, it's like a knife stuck into my heart.

Bill: We hope you won't be that stupid, but some of you may be thinking, just like Scott was...

Scott: It will never happen to me.

Bill: But it did happen to Scott, and he's had to suffer tremendous consequences.

Scott: And suffer I have.

Bill: One day he woke up in the hospital. He didn't know where he was, what had happened, or even what year it was.

Scott: I saw two people come into the room and they gestured to each other and pointed at me. I was terrified, but I couldn't move. They came closer to the bed and said…

Bill: Don't be afraid, we won't hurt you. We want to ask you a few questions. Do you care?

Scott: Like I was really in a position to argue.

Bill: Do you know your name?

Scott: I couldn't talk, but I could mouth the words.

Bill: Great, he knows his name.

Scott: I'd been Scott all my life! What's wrong with these people?

Bill: Do you know what happened to you?

Scott: I mouthed "drug overdose." I had been taking so much of so many different drugs that I figured if I ever ended up in a hospital, that would be why. I was stupid, sick, a loser. They said…

Bill: No, you were in a serious car accident.

Scott: That explained why I couldn't move a muscle. As Doctor Spock would say, it was logical.

Bill: One more question. Do you know what year it is?

Scott: I thought to myself, these people think I'm wacko because I knew it was 1989.

Bill: July 1990.

Scott: I had been in a coma for nine months. Wow!

Bill: Nine months. An entire school year. Thirty-nine weekends. Thanksgiving, Christmas, Easter, and the Fourth of July. His twenty-first birthday. Nine months.

Scott: All I could think was, "I want my mommy."

Bill: He couldn't talk for a whole year, unable to communicate feelings or needs.

Scott: The only thing I could do was blink my eyes once for "yes" and twice for "no."

Bill: Can you imagine how frustrating it was for a twenty-one-year-old man who couldn't do anything for himself?

Scott: This was a guy who was a super-jock. I even had to have people help me to go to the bathroom. I couldn't talk for about over a year, but now I won't shut up.

Bill: Scott went through a period when he didn't want to live anymore.

Scott: I knew I'd never play ball again.

Bill: But then he began to realize how precious life is...

Scott: And understand that playing ball is not everything.

Bill: Since his accident, Scott has had fourteen surgeries, on both legs, both arms, and both hands.

Scott: I haven't had surgery on my brain, but I've always needed that.

Bill: Things that everyone else takes for granted, Scott had to learn to do all over again. Things like eating, standing by himself, taking steps, talking.

Scott: I am heavily indebted to a rehabilitation unit named Rebound, located in Kansas City. The wonderful people there worked with me over two years in therapy, sometimes creating more pain than you can imagine—

Bill: In order to make his hands, arms, and legs function again.

Scott: At Rebound, I had a best friend. His name was Kenny. We both had head injuries and had a lot of trouble talking.

Bill: Kenny'd fallen two stories off a roof.

Scott: We came up with our own lingo—we were the only two who could understand what we were saying. We could talk about the nurses and then laugh. It drove them crazy.

Let me tell you about the brace I had to wear during my recovery.

Bill: Scott had to pre-stretch his arms before surgery.

Scott: It was the most painful thing of my recovery. Like bones just before they break. But they wouldn't take the braces off. I wanted to use a few choice words.

Bill: It was a major accomplishment for Scott when he was able to put on his own socks and shoes.

Scott: They told me, if I ever walked again, it would be a miracle. Guess what? Miracles happen.

Bill: His mom tells a story.

Scott: I'll tell you how much my mother loves me. When I was at Rebound, she drove 888 miles, fifteen hours, every weekend so I could come home.

Bill: The doctors told her the more Scott sees his old surroundings, the faster he will recover, so Beverly, even though it put a tremendous strain on her…

Scott: My mom made sure I was home as much as possible.

Bill: Beverly knew how much Scott wanted to walk on his own…

Scott: And prove the doctors wrong.

Bill: One day when he was home…

Scott: She peeked out the window and watched me walk—on my own—a third of a mile to my grandparents' house. The surprise and joy on their faces was worth the effort. On that day, Mom tells me, she knew I'd be okay.

Walking at Grandpa and Grandma's house.

Bill: Scott's older brother had a big surprise for him.

Scott: This really blew me away; my brother pushed me in my wheelchair into the garage at our house, and there was this bitchin' silver Camaro with a T-top. I said, "Cool, man, whose is that?" He said...

Bill: "It's yours."

Scott: I said, "No really, whose is it?"

Bill: "It's yours. Really. You had this car before the wreck. You were driving your work car. This was your party car."

Scott: I couldn't remember being the baseball MVP and I couldn't remember my most prized possession, that silver Camaro.

Bill: Scott has told you a little about the physical pain, but the emotional pain was new to him.

Scott: That was what really hurt. One night when I was in college at Iowa Western, at two-thirty in the morning, some fools, two guys and a girl, were drunk coming home from the bar, and thought it would be funny to harass me.

Bill: They pounded on his dorm room door...

Scott: Scared the hell out of me...

Bill: And said, "Na-na-na." Then they took off down the hall laughing.

Scott: I opened the door and yelled, "I love you," as loud as I could.

Bill: Which at that time wasn't much.

Scott: Outside the next day, I saw the woman walking to class. I yelled, "Hey, I know it was you."

Bill: She started walking faster.

Scott: I yelled again, "You can run from me, but not from God."

Bill: That stopped her. She came back to him and said...

Scott: "I'm sorry. That was stupid of us. You don't know how bad I feel."

Bill: And he said...

Scott: It's all forgiven. We all make mistakes.

Bill: Do you know why people do the wrong thing?

Scott: Because it's easy. Doing the right thing is hard.

Bill: Scott lifts weights now and he sort of enjoys the physical pain of lifting...

Scott: But nothing can compare to the emotional suffering of being laughed at and the butt of jokes.

Bill: Scott has turned into the type of person he used to dislike.

Scott: A good student.

Bill: When he attended Longview College in Grandview, Missouri, guess what?

Scott: I got straight A's. That's pretty good for a guy with two head injuries.

Bill: They said he'd never be able to learn again. Nevertheless, Scott graduated from Iowa Western in Council Bluffs with an Associate of Arts Degree in 1994.

There are no easy answers in life. Doing the right thing can be hard.

Scott: It hasn't been easy going from who I was to who I am, but I like myself now. One step further, I love myself now. If you can't love yourself, how can you expect someone else to?

Bill: Scott never has learned the easy way.

Scott: And I believe God saved me for a reason, to help young people learn from my mistakes.

Bill: In January of 1994, he legally changed his name to Scott McPhillips.

Scott: I wanted my real daddy's name.

Bill: And now he's a new person.

Scott: So you can call me Mac; all my friends do.

Bill: I know you've heard this before, but it's true and should be repeated as often as possible.

Scott: You don't need to drink or do drugs to make friends or have fun.

Bill: The consequences are too great.

Scott: Don't let what happened to me happen to you.

Bill: Friends may come and go throughout your life...

Scott: But your family is yours forever. When you get home, give them a big hug for me.

Bill: Don't take anything for granted, not your family, not sports, not life itself, not eternity.

Scott: When I was sitting where you are now, I was really good at doing the wrong thing. Look at where it got me.

Bill: Do the right thing.

Scott: Do it today. Procrastination is the assassination of motivation. Wow, that's a mouthful, but I just like saying it.

Bill: If you can't do it alone, then talk to someone else. See a teacher, a counselor, a minister. Talk to Sco—Mac after the program. Talk to your mom and dad. Talk to a friend and go get help together.

Scott: We all make mistakes. Don't let a mistake change your life forever.

Bill: Losers let it happen!

Scott: Winners make it happen! I was a loser and lousy things happened to me. Now I'm a winner. I'm taking control and g-r-e-a-t, great things are happening.

Bill: In the coming years, we'll probably read about someone drunk in a car accident. We'll probably read about someone spending months in a coma or someone who can only blink for "yes" and "no."

Scott: I don't ever want to read about you. I almost died. You don't have to. Be careful. Be safe. God has been my strength. And God bless you all.

Give the Gift of Inspiration to Your Friends and Colleagues

CHECK YOUR LEADING BOOKSTORE OR ORDER HERE

❑ YES, I want _____ copies of *Superman Doesn't Live Here Anymore* at $9.95 paperback or $14.95 hardcover, plus $3 shipping per book (Iowa residents please add $.60 paperback or $.90 hardcover sales tax per book). Canadian orders must be accompanied by a postal money order in U.S. funds. Allow 15 days for delivery.

My check or money order for $_____ is enclosed.
Please charge my ❑ Visa ❑ MasterCard

Name _____

Phone _____

Organization _____

Address _____

City/State/Zip _____

Card # _____

Exp. Date_____ Signature _____

Please make your check payable and return to:
Mac on the Attack for Jesus
28535 Coldwater Avenue
Honey Creek, IA 51542
Call your credit card order to: (712) 545-3003
Fax: (402) 572-4454
E-mail: bkrumwiede@aol.com

Daily Hope:
A Winter of Reflection

A Collection of Meditations for Your Spirit

VISION

Gathering...
Seeking the Source of Wholeness and Life
Longing to Quench a Common Thirst
Nurturing One Another.
In Community...
Being Filled and Renewed
Becoming Living Water
For Others in the World.

MISSION

*In response to God's grace and spirit, The Well offers spiritual
nourishment for daily living. Though grounded in Christianity,
the center reaches beyond denominations and traditions to provide
opportunities for spiritual growth and formation, equipping
individuals to serve God and others.*

Daily Hope: *A Winter of Reflection*
ISBN: 978-0-9829126-0-7
Copyright© 2010
Well for the Journey Publishing

Cover art by Becky Slater

Well for the Journey Publishing
a division of Well for the Journey, Inc.
7600 York Road
Towson, MD 21204
410-296-9355
www.wellforjourney.org
Email: info@wellforjourney.org

*Various translations of the Holy Bible are used throughout the text. For details
on the translation, please refer to the citations, found on pages 86 through 91.*

Introduction

Winter is often considered a fallow time – a time of bare trees and empty fields. But it is also a vital stage of growth and nourishment, and though little seems to be going on outside, a great deal is going on inside and in nature. For us, as well as for the natural world, this period of rest and nurture prepares us for the seasons ahead. Winter is the season in which we must trust in the hope of the new beginnings yet to come. Well for the Journey is delighted to offer *Daily Hope: A Winter of Reflection* as a resource for spiritual nourishment and reflection during the winter months.

Hope is a universal human experience that orients us to the future. Amidst the darkest time of the year, winter offers glimmers of divine hope – clear star-filled nights, family and friends gathered together, the strength and beauty of snow-draped evergreens. Yes, hope truly does shine within the darkness! As you move through the pages of this book, you are invited to begin each week with a brief guided reflection... to ponder the quotes and reflections... to journal with your thoughts and feelings... and to revisit the guided reflection at week's end to discover how God is at work in you.

It is my heartfelt prayer that *Daily Hope: A Winter of Reflection* will offer you encouragement, inspiration, and a sense of hope throughout the winter season.

Hope and peace to you,
Kathy Baker
Project Director
Daily Hope: A Winter of Reflection

Using this Book

Daily Hope: A Winter of Reflection is designed to be a daily resource for spiritual nourishment. The book is organized in seven-day cycles centered on a specific theme related to the spiritual life. On the first day, you are gently introduced to the week's theme by the word, "Pondering..." followed by questions which invite you to ponder the theme and consider how it relates to your life. For the next five days, you are offered quotes and reflections that resonate with the theme. The final day of the week begins with the words, "Echoes of..." This is a day to listen for the echoes of what you have experienced during the previous six days, and to discover and celebrate how God is at work in you. There is space on each page to write down your thoughts, if you so desire.

The writers and editors took great care to offer reflections that speak broadly about our encounters with God and the spiritual life. In order to address the wide diversity of approaches to the divine presence, it seems important to offer a few comments about the names we use to refer to "God." Each one of us has an individual, unique relationship with God, and many of us have our preferred name for our God. God may be "Father," "Mother," "Holy One," "Divine Power;" or simply unnamed. In order to offer a unifying tone to this book, as well as to recognize that our names for God are uniquely our own preference, we have decided, whenever possible, to use the recognized gender-neutral name "God." We hope that when you read the word "God," you will substitute your own name that best suits your relationship with God.

Pondering . . . Darkness

We are called to know and to name the gifts of the night and to share the visions that emerge from the darkness.
(Jan Richardson)

> The experience of darkness is often paradoxical.
> What feelings surface in your heart around darkness?
> How might darkness be a gift in your life?

This week explores nature's darkness as gift.

December 1

Arise, shine, for your light has come, and the glory of the Lord has dawned upon you. For behold, darkness covers the land; deep gloom enshrouds the peoples. But over you the Lord will rise, and his glory will appear upon you.

— Isaiah 60:1-3

Following diagnosis and treatment for cancer just over three years ago, I entered a period of darkness. My cancer was successfully cured through surgery, but lingering complications from surgery coupled with other life circumstances shrouded my outlook on life moving forward. During that period, which lasted over two years, this passage from Isaiah was enormously helpful and encouraging. I had recently learned to do watercolors, so I found myself "painting" this darkness in various abstract forms. In almost every painting I did in this "dark" period, light is emerging out of darkness.

I found myself enormously dependent on God during this time, for God was my Light in this darkness. That Light was constant and consistent, even when I was not. That dark time has now passed, and the Light continues to be as strong and as constant as ever. If darkness returns someday, I know that the Light will be there as well.

In Navajo culture, each day is greeted with a prayer to the sun as it rises in the day. God is my Sun. Darkness is vanquished by the continuous dawning of the glory of the Lord.

*I live my Advent in the womb of Mary...with hope's
expectance of nativity...I come upon earth's most amazing
knowledge: Someone is hidden in this dark with me.
Someone is hidden in this dark with me*

— Jessica Powers

The experience of darkness is such a powerful metaphor for mystery.
When it is dark, it is so hard to see, yet when I am in the dark about
things in my life, I most often learn to see more clearly. Darkness
often sparks fear within us, yet it is in the darkness of early morning
hours that I experience the shelter and safety of the Holy. It is in the
dark that most crimes are committed; yet it is within the darkness
of the womb and the darkness of the earth that new life is nurtured,
held safely, 'til it bursts forth in life. There can be no dawn without
darkness; no starlight visible to the human eye.

The darkness of winter invites me inside, not merely out of the cold,
but into the shadow places of my own heart. Here I can learn to rely
on senses other than sight --to "sense" into the wonder of my soul,
the wonder of my God-- to wait in "Mary-darkness" with the certainty
that the Holy is here with me.

If I say, "Surely the darkness shall cover me,
and the light around me become night,"
Even the darkness is not dark to you;
the night is as bright as day,
and the darkness is as light to you.

— Psalm 139:11-12

When I was eight and having a miserable year at school, darkness covered many of my days. We lived in a converted carriage house in an old farm complex. One winter evening, the children gathered to play games. Someone told a ghost story. At curfew, as I stepped into the darkness, alone, the wind swept me up in haunting laughter. I ran home, terrified and leaned into the safety of our front door to calm my breath. Sudden awareness of flickering lights though the branches of a tree stilled the scary voices. I stepped away from safety, out into the open to survey God's starry night.

Times of darkness are the times when we most need to look for hope. We find it often when we least expect it, as on a clear new-moon night when the stars light our way.

In the beginning when God created the heavens and the earth, the earth was a formless void and darkness covered the face of the deep, while a wind from God swept over the face of the waters. Then God said, "Let there be light," and there was light. And God saw the light and it was good.

— Genesis 1:1-4

What is good about the "light"? It offers vision and clarity to move from the darkness, but is that enough? Once we gain vision and clarity, we can smugly live a comfortable life in black and white. I say, vision and clarity are not enough! There has to be more when moving from darkness to light.

Ask yourself, how are we to respond to people whose lives are immersed in a shadow of darkness or are embroidered by a drapery of gray light? How are we called to respond when we encounter lives controlled by aggression, despair, anxiety, fear, hate, envy, competitiveness, or greed? How might we move beyond self-satisfied vision and clarity to respond to these questions?

With the light you possess, ignite the torch within your heart by knowing that the kingdom of God is within you. With that knowledge, the light which you carry will move you toward the colors of compassion, empathy, forgiveness, and striving for the common good. Ignite the torch and pass it.

> *Once the intellect is able to cross that chasm of terror,*
> *everything has changed forever.*
>
> —Alexander J. Shaia

Right here, darkness so dark, so deep.
An abyss, encapsulated.
Darkness wrapped.
Mysteriously. In more darkness.
Yet, only, right here,
The heart sees the naked soul.
God.
Dare not to look away.
And betray this sacred invitation.
To draw closer.
Peer intently, search the darkness, pursue the abyss.
Courageously.
Hold tenderly every emotion that awakens.
Nurture silently. Approach the Sacred.
Reverently.
To the depth and breadth of darkness.
Be.
In the moment of darkness.
Allow each tear to come, flood open the doorway.
Cross the threshold. Cross the chasm.
The deep. The abyss.
Found no other way, in no other place,
A moment, birthing and nourishing,
life of soul.
Lifting all grief, all fear. Lifting terror.
From this chasm, light delivers, love lives.
Holiness.
The eyes of the soul return a gaze
deep into the heart. Life changed forevermore.
This grace, enough.
Darkness, now, eternal hope.

Echoes of . . . Darkness

We are called to know and to name the gifts of the night and to share the visions that emerge from the darkness.
(Jan Richardson)

Thinking back on this week:
> How has darkness been a gift in your life?
> What changes do you notice within your heart in relation to darkness?
> How have you known the paradox of darkness?
> How does all this nurture hope in you?

Pondering . . . Fear

Do not be afraid, I am with you.
(Isaiah 41:10)

> "Fear not" is among the most quoted phrases in the Scriptures.
> What are the most common fears you hold in your heart?
> What are your images of fear?
> How does fear hold you back? Challenge you to move forward?

This week, hear the Holy One speak "Fear not" over your fears.

December 8

...and we looked like grasshoppers to ourselves, and so we must have looked to them.

One of the many commentaries on this passage suggests that the people are afraid to enter the land of milk and honey because they are afraid to leave what is known for what is unknown. How many times does this same attitude affect our ability to take a chance and thereby reap some great benefit? When reflecting on the impact of this hesitancy versus courage in my own life, I am reminded of the times when I have been afraid to move forward, afraid to leave the known behind for the unknown. Whether it is a major decision such as a marriage, a cross-country move, or a smaller decision, such as committing to a volunteer position, we must allow ourselves to feel the fear of the unknown, but not let that fear guide our decision-making. It is at these times that we must hone our ability to listen to our "gut instinct" – that inner voice that God uses to gently nudge us. How is God speaking to you through your inner voice, your "gut instinct"? How is God encouraging you to leap into the unknown? Your reward for courageously leaping? The Promised Land.

"As long as we see ourselves merely as grasshoppers up against giants, we will set ourselves up for failure. If we want to create anything new and to enter into the Promised Land, then we have no choice but to leap into the unknown, to believe in ourselves, and to trust in God's faith in us."   (Cantor Josee Wolfe)

12   **Daily Hope:** *A Winter of Reflection*

Courage is fear that has said its prayers.

— Dorothy Bernard

Rarely a day that goes by that I do not encounter fear. Fear of being embarrassed, of seeming unprepared, or of letting others down; of having a difficult conversation with a family member or co-worker, of getting out of a comfort zone and trying something new, of confronting an injustice – these are some of the fears I often experience.

I have found prayer to be a wonderful antidote for fear. When I take the time to pray about a situation, event, or person that triggers fear, I always seem to have a greater sense of confidence or serenity, whatever the outcome may be. Prayer works best when I do not ask for a desired result, but only that God walk hand-in-hand with me and lead me to react or respond in a way that would please God and be consistent with God's will. Walking with God, I can face any fear.

Blessed is the one who is fearful always.

— Proverbs 28:14

We are under the impression that fear is to be avoided. In fact, President Franklin D. Roosevelt famously suggested that fear is the only thing to fear. According to King Solomon, however, it is a blessing to be fearful. To what fear does this proverb refer? How are we to truly fear?

We fear the uncertainty of the future. In response, we often attempt to manage the fear with control, believing that by controlling every aspect of our lives we can orchestrate future outcomes. This control creates a false sense of security which misleadingly diminishes the fear. As President Roosevelt noted, it is this type of fear that we should fear.

The proverb instructs us to use fear as a tool for growth. We can manage fear with control or face fear with faith. Ultimately, the future is uncertain regardless of our attempts to control it. The only way to truly be at ease with fear of the future is to place our faith in God – the One who truly controls the future. It is this type of fear –a fear that leads to faith– that King Solomon considers a blessing.

God has not given us a spirit of fear, but of power, and of love, and of a sound mind.

— 2 Timothy 1:7

When I am afraid, the fear usually originates with my thoughts, leading to worry about the unknown, the "what if's" of my imagination. What if I do not have enough money to retire, what if the pain in my back does not go away, and what if I am too sore or tired to complete the projects I have started?

At times like these, I remind myself that I am not alone; God is at my side guarding, protecting, enlightening, and encouraging, and all shall be well. I stop, eat to gain strength, rest, and begin anew. In the morning, in the light of day when all is fresh and new, I see more clearly. Enlightenment often comes after sleep, prayer, stillness, and quiet.

A sense of peace ensues as I become aware of God's ever present love for me, as well as the God-given strength, wisdom, and clear thinking that allow me to discover solutions to any pressing problem. Patiently and methodically, I focus on one step at a time, keeping my mind from jumping to unknown steps ahead, where worry and fear lie. Trusting God, trusting myself, and trusting others brings inner peace and puts all my fears to rest.

It is a time of change, the saving hour!
The word is not fear, the word we live, but an old word
suddenly made new as we learn it again,
as we bring it alive: LOVE, LOVE, LOVE, LOVE.

— May Sarton

Sociologists tell us that we live in a culture of fear. Rapid change, constant unknowing, terrorism, invisible enemies, economic instability –to name just a few– feed our fear daily. The Scripture passages of Advent and Christmas are filled with the recognition of how prevalent fear is in the human heart. To Mary, the angel says, "Fear not...." Those same words are echoed to Joseph, to shepherds in the field, to wise ones seeking the Holy. They are among the most quoted words in all of the Bible. As a former teacher, I know that repetition is a strong teaching tool. How persistent the Divine Teacher is that we get the message!

Fears abounded 2000 years ago in the Roman-controlled region of Bethlehem. A young girl had the courage to say "Yes" in spite of the threat of death for one pregnant and unmarried. A young man trusted love enough to believe in dreams. Wise ones foolishly travelled far from home seeking an infant king. Justifiable and real fears.

Yet LOVE took the risk to be born in the midst of it all. So fear not!

Echoes of . . . Fear

Do not be afraid, I am with you.
(Isaiah 41:10)

Looking back on the week:
    What changes do you notice within you in relation to fear?
    What lessons has fear taught you this week?
    Continue to attune the ear of your heart to the repetition of
        "fear not" in the Scriptures of this season.
    How does all this nurture hope in you?

Pondering . . . Silence and Stillness

Because God whispers. . . .being silent means more than just holding your tongue. It means listening for the softest, most subtle sound of all – the sound of the soul.
(Tijn Touber)

We live in a culture of non-stop noise ...
    What part do silence and stillness play in your life?
    What are your feelings and images around silence and stillness?
    How do you recognize the 'sound of your soul'?

This week, listen for the sounds of silence around you.

Silence is the mother of truth.

— Benjamin Disraeli

I was fortunate to know silence as a young girl. My "baptism" to its practice came on a sunny day that held only the necessary crispness to make it fall; it was Thanksgiving and I was not yet a teenager.

The table had been set, the turkey basted, and the potatoes that would be mashed had begun to boil. I was given permission to walk alone to the woods at the end of my street. More than fifty years ago it was safe to do this, though I was warned not to go beyond the stream.

There, after a short walk, I sat quietly on a tumbled tree trunk wearing blue jeans and a flannel shirt, and understood for the first time that there was something that was greater than all that I knew. Later, my stillness came as a spirit that I could grab onto in order to focus my busy mind and listen and learn from the words of others.

Today, I find this peace whether sitting in my reading chair or walking my dog. And it is in this silence and stillness that I reconcile the conflicts of mind and heart and continue to learn the truths of my existence.

Be still and know that I am God.

— Psalm 46:10

Throughout my life, I, like most of us, have worn many hats: that of wife, mother, daughter, friend, community and charity volunteer. Frequently, at day's end, after the children were bathed and bedded, I'd ask my husband to give me just a few minutes of quiet before we'd settle down to catch up with the day's events. My arms were simply too tired from changing hats.

I enjoyed motherhood and I've never been one to spend much time focused on future, but somehow, in the deep recesses of my mind, I believed that things would get easier as the children grew. I'd have fewer demands on my time. Not so. My roles have expanded to grandmother, writer, businesswoman, single homeowner, and caregiver to older adults in my life. Frequently, I feel that old weariness of changing hats. Then I know that it is time to escape to that place where my role never changes, to the silence of my faith where I utter quietly and slowly: "Be still and know that I am God."

December 17

There is simply an indescribable intensity of absorption into what I can only call the immensity of God.

— Sr. Jeremy Hall, OSB

In a natural bowl, circled by the Allegheny Mountains, sits the National Radio Astronomy Observatory. The observatory is surrounded by 13,000 square miles designated as a Radio Quiet Zone. Among the array of equipment, the largest scope stands 43 stories. It supports a 2.3 acre collecting dish surfaced with 2,000 panels. Each panel is adjustable to within a hundred millionths of a meter. The purpose of the scopes is to listen intently to the immensity of deep space.

In a rocker, in a house in Baltimore City, surrounded by the stuff of daily life, sits a 5 foot, 6 inch woman. Without benefit of a Quiet Zone, she tries to orient her personal collecting dish to the awareness of the presence of God. The two main panels on her dish, Past and Future, resist fine-tuning. But, once in a while, intentionally or inadvertently, the woman fixes on a single point – the sensation of her breath, the view through bare branches, the whisper of falling snow. As her attention settles, a curtain opens in the fabric of the cosmos. There, a step through the curtain, and she is welcomed into Now, the place and space of God.

Be silent.
Be still.
Let your God
Look upon you.
That is all.

— Edwina Gateley

Edwina Gateley wrote those words in 1979 in the silence and stillness of a three month stay in a small stone hermitage in the Algerian desert. I live alone, and it is easy to be silent and still—or is it?

The noise outside my window—cars passing, birds singing, children walking to school—is easily blocked from my consciousness, unless it is an ambulance, which, even after nine years, takes me back to the night my husband died. It is the noise inside my head that distracts me from awareness of God's compassionate gaze. As I sit at prayer, a thought for later in the day intrudes. Where is my pen? If I capture the thought, will it go away until I finish talking to God? The intrusion may not keep me so much from talking to God as to listening for the still small voice that lets me know when God responds. My hope, each day, is for awareness of the wonder of this conversation.

God addresses us not when we are babbling away about Him or even primarily to Him, but when we remain silent—not only when we refrain from speech, glances and gestures, but when we allow thoughts to become still and emotions calm.

— Donald Spoto

I love sitting outside on my patio, especially when a breeze continually rings the chimes that hang from the rainspout. If I am still, a chipmunk may race under my chair and scamper quickly up the steps to surprise me. On summer and fall days, deer will wander into the yard, munching ivy within ten feet of me. They look at me, taking in the curiosity that I must be, and then start munching again. The birds fly in and out of the feeder unless, of course, the squirrels have taken up residence. In late summer, butterflies will come and sometimes even land on my lap! In winter, I look out and sigh as the snow settles all down to stillness.

Stillness, the quiet sitting and being, allows me to become aware of the life that is around me. Something of God shouts aloud in these moments. I hear the laughter of God in all creation. I bask in the calm and peace of rest. I settle into a grace-filled time of reflection and pondering. I sense new ways of thinking and being. I love knowing God is glad that I took some time to sit in the stillness of the Holy Presence.

Echoes of . . . Silence and Stillness

Because God whispers....being silent means more than just holding your tongue. It means listening for the softest, most subtle sound of all – the sound of the soul.
(Tijn Touber)

Looking back on this week:
    What gifts of silence and stillness did you discover?
    Were you able to hear the 'sound of your soul'?
    How do you recognize the sounds of silence?
    How does all this nurture hope in you?

Pondering . . .Wonder

Each new day is a path of wonder, a different invitation.
(John O'Donohue)

What do you wonder about?
    What moves your heart to wonder?
    What things give you pause to wonder?
    Who are those who teach you how to live with a spirit of
    wonder and surprise?

Be open to wonder this week....in all the unexpected places!

We love the Lord, of course, but we often wonder what He finds in us.

— Edgar Watson Howe

I wonder about Heaven
And about Hell.
Pondering the Entrance
Or the flaming swell.

Will Peter say "Welcome!"
Or "Sorry, Nice try"?
I wonder if there's a checklist
Or will I just get by.

I wonder about comparisons
And measuring up.
Some deeds are depleting
And some fill my cup.

I wonder about actions of ego
That guide some choices;
Not listening with heart.
Where are the voices?

I wonder about Faith
And its draw on me.
Mystery, questions remain
For the life I was meant to be.

Tell me, what is it you plan to do with your one wild and precious life?

— Mary Oliver

Wonder: astonishment at something awesomely mysterious or new to one's experience; exciting amazed admiration; a feeling of doubt or uncertainty; perceiving something rare or unexpected; surprise.

It's in our nature - we love the unexpected experience of wonder in life. With anticipation, we live to be awed. In our waiting, we look mostly outside of who we are for the spectacular! Living these winter months, however, when life turns inward – hibernation calls the wild to sleep; tree life happens underfoot; we retreat into the warmth of home; darkness squeezes daylight's appearance a bit more each day – do we dare look inward? Will we experience wonder there?

Will we be astonished with the awesome mysteries by which we're created? Will we experience amazing admiration as we gaze upon our own soul? Will we celebrate the beauty and rarity fashioned within us? Will we be awed by the surprising potential revealed as we see ourselves with the eyes of God? And in the darkness of doubt and uncertainty, can wonder's light shine?

It is in darkness when light shines the brightest! Do you dare believe that God's heart jumps as the Creator gazes upon the wonder of the created...you?

Consider the thousands of miles of earth beneath your feet;
think of the limitless expanse of space above your head.
Walk in awe, wonder, and humility.

—Wilferd A. Peterson

On our two week road trip out west, my family spent a day mountain biking through the magnificent Grand Teton National Park in Wyoming. Early on, I was overwhelmed with excitement and, pedaling quickly, my eyes looked upon a perfect blend of lodgepole pines, red flowers, bald eagles, and snow-capped mountains. It was a sight more magnificent than anything I had ever seen. We suddenly halted to allow a herd of bison to cross in front of us. They jumped over fences on either side of the path, running into the depths of the Tetons with an incredulous grace for such massive animals. Being so close to such spectacular creatures made me feel like one small piece of nature's huge puzzle. As the trip wound down, we stopped to rest in front of a picturesque cabin, set at the base of the grandest mountain in the range, where lush fields of gold and green rolled out to greet the wooden structure. Awestruck by the vastness of nature, I slowly pedaled back, filled with a deepened appreciation of the earth.

To be surprised, to wonder, is to begin to understand.

— Jose Ortega y Gasset

Peeking out slowly
Dim at first
But growing brighter
Flickering night light
Soon joined by many others.

Jewels of the heavens
Sparkling brightly
Lighting the way
        For the Magi
        For the slaves
        For the mariner
        For the wanderer.

May we ever wonder
How you were placed
By the hand of God
Set gently down
To light the way
If we will but follow.

Open our eyes
To the stars that guide us
Let their light be a comfort
In times of darkness
And draw us ever closer to you.

I wonder as I wander out under the sky,
How Jesus the Savior did come for to die.

— John Jacob Niles

Ah, the wonderment and beauty of a winters' night. How many of us never really ever experience it? We're snuggled up inside under a warm blanket, a fire blazing, and a movie playing on the television. Our goal is to remain far from the elements and cold outside. Sure, we might look out the window to gaze at the snow. But, more often than not, we're doing everything humanly possible to remain warm and cozy. We fix big, hearty meals to comfort our souls and turn the thermostat up high. And we hibernate within our homes and within ourselves. Can you imagine walking alone on a freezing-cold night, just reflecting and thinking about God?

We may force ourselves out into the cold night air to walk the dog or shovel the snow. But, just out wandering and wondering? Probably not. Being alone and surrounded by God's beauty brings wonderment – it is thought provoking. In today's busy, self-centered world, it is rare that we take a quiet, peaceful journey alone to think and ponder. True solitude mixed with deep thought takes planning and practice. It requires discipline. It is something I don't often do. But, it is something that we all must do in order to have a full appreciation of our faith and God's wonderful creation.

Echoes of . . .Wonder

Each new day is a path of wonder, a different invitation.
(John O'Donohue)

Reflecting back on this week:
    What was "wonder-full" in these days?
    Who were those who taught you how to wonder?
    What did you "wonder" about?
    How does all this nurture hope in you?

Pondering . . . Mystery and the Unknown

The most beautiful thing we can experience is the mysterious.
(Albert Einstein)

    What are those things that draw your heart into mystery?
    How at rest is your heart in the unknown?
    Is there mystery in your heart that God desires
        to shed light upon?

Let your life unfold in mystery this week. Walk confidently into the
new year!

Almighty God, unto whom all hearts are open, all desires known, and from whom no secrets are hid . . .

— Book of Common Prayer

God knows our secrets but we can only glimpse God's mystery slant-wise, out of the corner of the eye, as it were, or in the moment between waking and sleep when clarity is not a quality of light but of darkness.

A woman comes to Jesus, with a jar of costly ointment; she weeps so copiously that she washes his feet with her tears; she pours the ointment over his feet. Jesus, who knows the thoughts of the disapproving Pharisee who watches this scene, also knows the secrets of this woman. She has sinned greatly, he says, and she is forgiven of all her sins.

The real mystery in the story is not the nature of her sins, not the scope of her sins, not the duration of her sins. The real mystery is not that Jesus knows all about her. The real mystery is that she is forgiven and she knows it. She comes to Jesus not to ask for forgiveness, but to give thanks for forgiveness.

The real mystery is that God enters our lives and transforms them and only then –when we feel ourselves transformed– do we realize that God has been at work. The real mystery is God's grace, abundant and beyond price.

There are moments when healing takes place in our lives and the only way we can explain the healing is by living it.

— Macrina Wiederkehr

God's work in me has always been a mystery. Having experienced a lot of personal loss and relationship issues, I've been told by a professional that I need to reach a place of "beautiful sadness." This "beautiful sadness" is a place of quiet acceptance where I know I can't fix anything. It is a realization that sadness and brokenness are a part of life, and that I can take in the things that are beautiful in spite of the sadness.

How to arrive at this place is a mystery to me. This is where I believe I need to open myself and invite God in. I don't understand how God's loving powers heal me, but I do know that without them, I will never reach "beautiful sadness." I pray that by the grace of God, profound changes will happen deep in my heart. There is no easy way to deal with the difficulties in my life, but with God's help, I am open to the mystery that helps me journey closer to this place of "beautiful sadness."

The mystery never leaves you alone.

– John O'Donohue

"Mystery" is one of my favorite words for God. In my heart, I know we can never truly understand the nature of God. We get only glimpses. We wrestle with eternal questions such as: "Where are you, God?" "Why is there suffering?" "What is my purpose?" These questions cannot –in this lifetime– be answered in a way that satisfies us. Answers unfold slowly and subtly. As small particles of life in the vast space of time, we experience tiny moments that offer insight into our mysterious God.

Yet, I live in the here and now of daily life. I was professionally trained to provide answers, minimize risk, and be efficient. Contemporary culture encourages us to conquer all the questions. We need practical information to live, love, and work.

The challenge, then, is to live gently in the tension – to embrace the mystery and the practicalities of daily life. Every day, I seek to balance my heart and my head. And as I continue to be drawn into the big questions, I discover that if I pay attention to life, bits of the answers are revealed in small, unexpected ways. I just need to get more comfortable with the unknowable – with living into the mystery.

In my room, the world is beyond my understanding,
But when I walk out I see that it
consists of three or four hills and a cloud.

— Wallace Stevens

During seasons of prolonged hours of daylight, my spiritual life is a natural response to God and creation. It seems to be connected so closely to nature through the beauty of flowers, lush green surroundings, hummingbirds, chipmunks, and outside activities that it is as much a part of my being as the air I breathe.

As daylight hours shorten, however, my hours of productivity begin to wane and I feel a sense of loss. My energy level drops, and I tend to crawl into myself to regain balance and wholeness. I experience lethargic moments of disconnection and fragmentation. My soul feels tired and uncertain.

It isn't until I take a deep breath and surrender myself to the effects of winter's relative darkness that I begin to deal with the stripped down versions of my spiritual sources. I must go deeper. I need to understand how barren trees tell a story of courageous beauty as they rise and outline their strength against backdrops of vividly painted sunsets. In their stark unadorned appearance, they hold the mystery of eternity.

January 2

> *We're not afraid of losing time but of having time to reflect. Without the usual distractions and interference, we may have to confront feelings of disappointment, loneliness, frustration, panic, helplessness, and exhaustion, and our fear that we are not strong enough to make the changes we need to make.*
>
> — Wendy Mogel

My life often feels as though the days are strung together, going from one errand to the next; the different days marked by which item gets crossed off the to-do list. There's something satisfying about marking things off the list. That feeling of accomplishment rivals no other – a measure of success: if I can ever finish all the tasks, then I'll finally feel fulfilled!

My 4 year old constantly reminds me, however, that the to-do list means little when it comes to the holy and mysterious purpose of life. She's asking questions: "Who is God?" "Is God a she or a he?" "Is God strong enough to lift up the earth?" Poignant questions that point to where she is developmentally, and to how far away I've gotten from where I could be, spiritually.

If I had more time, I might accomplish more of the items on my list. But I wouldn't necessarily have better responses to her questions. No amount of rushing around puts me in a better place to engage these questions of mystery with her or with myself.

The days of winter –with holiday celebrations, school events, and the myriad other tasks to be done– can pass by quickly. Perhaps we can allow ourselves to take a few things off our to-do lists and sit, with no agenda and no purpose, to ponder in amazement the mystery of God.

Echoes of . . . Mystery and the Unknown

The most beautiful thing we can experience is the mysterious.
(Albert Einstein)

As you look back on this week:
    What steps into mystery did you find yourself taking?
    Do you recognize new clarities?
    What beauty did you discover in mystery and unknowing?
    How does all this nurture hope in you?

January 4

Pondering . . . Hearth and Home

Make me your home, as I have made you my home.
(John 15:4, adapted)

    What images come to mind as you reflect on hearth and home?
    What are the blessings for you that rest in hearth and home?
    Who or what brings you home to your heart?

Be aware this week of the place of home and hearth in your life.

You can't always get what you want. But if you try sometimes, you might find you get what you need.

— Mick Jagger and Keith Richards

Many of my God moments –moments when I am aware of the Holy Spirit's presence– happen in my car, usually while I am listening to WYPR. On "The Diane Rehm Show," a married couple, American educators teaching in Africa, described their careers and nomadic lifestyle. They relocated frequently to various countries within the continent. It required them to live with few possessions. To create a hearth in their transient world, they created a must-have list: a candle, a favorite photo, and fresh flowers. The couple explained that they could create a home anywhere, once their must-haves were displayed. As I listened in my car while running my errands, I thought about my must-haves. What are they?

In my adolescent days, I needed Mick Jagger's face in my home. His posters were omnipresent. As an adult, my must-haves are less about possessions and more about feelings. My must-haves are light and warmth. My home must have warm colors and lots of natural light. My must-haves invite love, hospitality, and security.

What are your must-haves?

January 6

*A life without love in it is like a heap of ashes upon a
deserted hearth... Life has taught us that love does not
consist in gazing at each other but in looking outward
together in the same direction.*

— Antoine de Saint-Exupery

The first time I went with my very Irish mother to visit her home in Ireland, my grandmother, or "Granny," was still alive. Each evening, she would light a peat fire in the fireplace. The family would sit around this fire and just enjoy being with one another. The simple pleasure of just being together, enjoying one another's company without the noise of the television in the background, is a lost treasure. I sometimes sense discomfort if there is no sound other than the voices of those treasuring the time together.

There is a sense of warmth when family or friends sit together and share their day, their concerns, their joys, and their sorrows. When we can talk to those we trust about our troubles, a sense of relief comes over us. While our problems may not go away, we can move forward, "looking outward," with loved ones by our side.

We may not always have a fire to sit beside, but hopefully there is a fire of love within us to ease our concerns and illuminate our joys. Be at peace with your home fire.

But there's no need to worry
this is just a vacation
it's not permanent leaving...

— Animal Collective

It would bubble up into my thoughts and repeat over and over again in my head; a mantra, or almost a dirge. I would be at the dinner table at home with my parents or driving to meet a friend, and it would seep into me, the awareness that I would be leaving again soon – leaving to return to a place that I would have given anything to leave behind forever. But as these thoughts surged, I was also comforted by the chant. Its beat reminded me that I was coming home again soon, that I could make it through the leaving until my next return. I could make it through all the leavings, until the school year was through.

Home is where your story begins.

— Annie Danielson

He startled me. While watering my holly tree, I noticed a perfectly formed bird nest resting on the branches. It was tiny, but beautifully constructed. And then I saw him -- a baby bird on a nearby branch, staring at me, motionless, except for his tiny blinking eyes. The hint of a breeze ruffled the scraggly new feathers on the top of his head. I assured him that I was simply caring for his home, watering the tree that held his nest, and that I would not hurt him. His eyes never left mine. I told him how beautiful he was, and how his parents had wisely chosen a wonderful place for him to live and grow. It was an amazing moment of connection between human and nature.

The encounter reminded me of my home, and how as a parent, I am responsible for creating a safe, nurturing environment for my own children. Home really is where your story begins. May our home be filled of tales of love, support, warmth, and encouragement. May my children be open to nurturing in its many forms, with the wide-eyed wonder of a baby bird.

Every day is a journey, and the journey itself is home.

— Matsuo Basho

Our home is warmed by the familiarity of those whom we love and with objects that kindle memories of people we care for and events we have enjoyed. Home gives us a safe place to be ourselves, to explore what it means to be our true selves. Home is a womb: a place to be nourished and rejuvenated.

Sometimes, though, the house we call home is a place of fear, full of monsters and bad memories, a place from which we need to escape to feel safe. It is in these times that we must journey further, in search of a safer, more nurturing refuge.

The journey of our days is home. Our journey leads us deep inside ourselves. Our journey guides us to those who love us, who share in our joys and sorrows. Our journey involves seeking God and recognizing God's loving presence. We create places and encounter people we call "home." For it is there we find the blazing hearth of God's spirit or the soft glowing ember of God's constant, unwavering love. Home, then, is wherever the divine energy of God meets the divine energy in our soul. Within the arms of God we are truly home.

When at peace, I am home.
When with you, I am home.
With you, God, I am home.

Echoes of . . . Hearth and Home

Make me your home, as I have made you my home.
(John 15:4, adapted)

Reflecting back on this week:
    In what ways has the concept of hearth and home changed or
        grown within you?
    Where in your heart are you most at home now?
    How does all this nurture hope in you?

Pondering . . .Waiting

Somewhere, something incredible is waiting to be known.
(Blaise Pascal)

What is the experience of waiting like for you?
    What are you waiting for now, at this time in your life journey?
    What does this time in nature say to you about waiting?
    Who or what supports you in your "waiting times"?

This week, be attentive to circumstances that make you wait...
and watch how you do it!

... in many ways, waiting is the missing link in the transformation process ...

— Sue Monk Kidd

In the waiting time
the time between what was
and what will be
the time of unknowing
of fear and hope and dread and joy
God is waiting with us.

In the waiting time
we call upon our Lord
knowing that God hears us
and that the waiting time will move
moment by moment
day by day
darkness to light
sadness to joy.

The spiritual life is a life in which we wait, actively present to the moment, trusting that new things are far beyond our own imagination, fantasy, or prediction.

— Henri Nouwen

Waiting is challenging, particularly when we encounter times that, no matter how hard we try, we are unable to change our situation. Frustration shadows our sense of imagination, and we are left feeling stagnate.

Yet life teaches that in the moments of struggle, when things seem most dormant, there are seeds of new growth which lie beneath the surface, watered by hope and warmed by love, waiting and working to emerge. Sometimes it is the words of others who have been there before, encouraging us to try something new or to put down what binds us. Sometimes it is the internal whisper of the Spirit drawing us away from that which diminishes life and drawing us into the light of hopefulness.

Let the season be a reminder that the promise of spring lies in every snowflake that falls, blanketing and nourishing what is yet to burst forth. And so we wait, listening and watching for signs of new life, trusting that the gardener of our souls is always at work beneath the surface.

*But those who wait for the Lord shall renew their strength,
they shall mount up with wings like eagles, they shall run
and not be weary, they shall walk and not faint.*

— Isaiah 40:31

I'm not a very patient person, a fact that seems especially apparent when I wait for something. Right now I'm waiting for a cake to bake, and I can hardly stand it! Waiting for the arrival of my babies seemed so long; I called my clothes eternity clothes! Nine months to meet and embrace the children I had always loved and longed for took a lot of patience and faith.

I now await a crisis, possibly a death, which is stressful and emotionally draining. My parents are struggling through the final chapter of their lives, one with multiple health issues and one with Alzheimer's. They live on their own as we search for homes able to care for their particular needs. Each time I leave them, I feel I've left a toddler and sick grandfather with impaired mobility in a war zone. It is in God's hands. I rest in the hope that they will be lifted out of their suffering, peacefully waiting to be joined by their loved ones left behind, and will be together again, happy and whole. Peaceful anticipation.

While practicing patience amidst this sadness, I am able to find hidden blessings. Together with thoughtful, prayerful friends and family, we discover ways to lighten some of the dark moments with occasional laughter, often interspersed with tears, cleansing tears. God's presence is palpable.

Waiting is, by its nature, something only the humble can do with grace.

— John Ortberg

Why is it so hard to let go and wait humbly for outcomes? It would seem I have lived long enough –and waited often enough– to realize that there is a drop off point when any further form of stressful behavior on my part is self defeating. I have filled, and utilized the tools in my box of strategies to combat anxiety. I have stayed busy, read, reflected, exercised, used deep breathing techniques, and prayed. Yet when I awake at 3:00 in the morning, still troubled, I am annoyed with myself. I have left out an important piece of the process. I have not trusted God to take over while I sleep. I have forgotten that I am not in control all the time. I need to back off. I need to let God be God.

With the energy we have, we begin the day,
waiting and watching and hoping.
We wait, not clear about our waiting.
But filled with a restlessness,
daring to imagine that you are not finished yet . . .

—Walter Brueggemann

Waiting. An alien way of being for our nanosecond world. Waiting, however, is inevitable. Waiting visits us daily – at a stoplight, in a checkout line, for a computer program to load. Then there are those periods when we've been waiting for years. Waiting comes quietly and in stillness, while at other times it roars with a storm of emotions – confusion, impatience, anger, restlessness, grief. The question then comes, "What will we do with this presence of waiting?"

Our desire is to banish waiting time in order to get on with our life! But what if our life can be found within the waiting? We abide, then, in the tension of waiting within the restlessness that dares us to imagine –not fleeing this discomfort too quickly, but to be awake and aware– waiting for the Spirit to lead, to blow through us, pulling us toward an encounter with the Holy, God's invitation to deeper intimacy where we are invited to learn the ways of trusting. And when the waiting is too long, too draining, and our trust has melted away, we then lean on others to trust for us.

Embrace the gift of waiting! Embrace the restlessness! Dare to imagine! Know that God is working on your behalf even when you are unaware. And know this: in the shadows of uncertainty, there is this truth and hope. You are not finished yet.

Echoes of . . .Waiting

Somewhere, something incredible is waiting to be known.
(Blaise Pascal)

Looking back on these days:
 What did you learn about yourself this week?
 Who were your teachers?
 What "gifts worth waiting for" did you discover this week?
 How does all this nurture hope in you?

Pondering . . . Questioning

...have patience with all that is unresolved in your heart and try to love the questions themselves.
(Rainer Maria Rilke, adapted)

 What are the deepest questions of your heart?
 What have you learned from your questioning -
  of life, of spirit, of love, of hope?
 "Quest" is part of questioning. How have your questions
  provided a path for you?

Follow your questions this week with curiosity.

You don't want a million answers as much as you want a few forever questions. The questions are diamonds you hold in the light. Study a lifetime and you see different colors from the same jewel.

— Richard Bach

For a while now, I have been asking God, "Who do you say that I am?" One night, I got a glimpse into the answer...

Outside in the chilly, winter evening, the wind whipped around me, then swirled up through the pine trees. I found myself wishing I could fly like Peter Pan: I had the oddest sensation that if I opened my arms wide, I could soar up into the dark sky. I needed this time in the dark, with the wind swirling and the moon rising in the inky, blue sky. God, in this night, called me to remember who I am, not just a wife, a mother, a daughter, a sister, and a friend, but who I am deep down, my authentic self – the person God created me to be. I stood up, walked over to the giant pine trees at the edge of the driveway and looked up at their branches waving in the wind. It was as if they were dancing, and for a brief, slightly self-conscious moment, I raised my hands to the sky and swayed with the trees, joining the dance of the wild night.

Tonight, I know this: I am the beloved child of a wonderful and creative God who chose to reach out and speak deeply to me through the stark beauty of a winter's night. And it is good.

Don't turn your head. Keep looking at the bandaged place.
That's where the light enters you. And don't believe for a
moment that you're healing yourself.

— Rumi

The Meeting House bench. The seventh pew on the left side of the small church where I first felt close to God and to myself. My car, with the music pumping so loudly that it hugs me close and all I can feel is relief and peace, and all I can do is accept the grace of the moment. My faith and my spirit feel so strong in these moments that I don't question them.

It is in the other moments – the ones where I am curled up in a dark, doubting hole of myself that I do. There are times that I cannot reach that light within myself and really don't even want to try. It takes a moment of breathtaking brilliance, the kind found on benches, in pews, and in cars, allowing the Light to shine within, to know that it never had any doubts about me.

The important thing is not to stop questioning.

—Albert Einstein

Really? What about the importance of being decisive and making Mom-Dad-Employee-Boss "commando" decisions? Being merely mortal, I do not question the brilliance of Professor Einstein, or any of the other great questioners of our day or of the past (think of Socrates' method), but my days are typically a blur, start to finish (kids, work, boss, kids, errands, too little sleep), so it's very easy to skip the questioning part.

So often the big questions, the ones to mull and ponder, fall by the wayside. Who has the time? Who has the patience? I must tend to the nitty-gritty of here and now, because the other questions consume my attention: What am I throwing together for dinner tonight? What time is [fill-in-the-blank] practice? Did you do your homework? Did you finish the report/brief/paper on time for the Board/court/class? I look forward to the luxury of time when I can ponder such big questions as:

What is my calling in life?
What does God want me to do?
How can I help?
Here are my hands, how will You use them?

> *The creative individual has the capacity to free himself from the web of social pressures in which the rest of us are caught. He is capable of questioning the assumptions that the rest of us accept.*
>
> — John W. Gardner

When young children ask one question after another, some adults can become frustrated. Children learn about the world through their personal experiences as well as having their many questions answered. Their questioning is a sign of their authenticity and fullness of life.

That should be true of adults as well. As young people, many of us were taught that it was rude to ask questions or that asking questions betrayed our ignorance or skepticism, particularly about matters of faith. But that's not necessarily the case. Consider all the persons in the Bible who questioned God, and consider all the times that God questioned various individuals!

The key to questioning is humility: we don't assume that we know the answers, and we recognize the limitations of our knowledge or opinions. We seek to learn, not to show others up. When we are truly receptive to new insights and information from the answers to our questions, we begin to see with fresh eyes and hear with fresh ears. And it is precisely in this "new" seeing and hearing that we who strive to pose honest and thoughtful questions become our most authentic selves.

...he said to them, "Peace be with you"... Then he said, "Why are you troubled...why do questions arise in your hearts?"

— Luke 24:36-38

Questions are how we learn, how we come to know. Our inquisitiveness is God's gift. But in the realm of faith, we may think questions are wrong, even sinful.

But what is faith if not belief in what we cannot know? If we claim to "know" in matters of faith, we go back to humanity's fall –the desire to know as God knows– and that is not of God.

We needn't be troubled by questions in our hearts. We need only give voice to them in prayer. Abraham, Moses, Job, the Psalmists – all brought their questions to God. Jesus, at the height of suffering, called out: "Why have you abandoned me?"

It is often easy to see God in joyous times, but it is in the throes of doubt, fear, or grief that questions about God arise. The very time we most need God is the time we may feel God's absence. Crying out, bringing my questions to God, are my most fruitful prayer experiences.

I receive the "answer" of peace when I have the courage to ask the questions.

Echoes of . . . Questioning

...have patience with all that is unresolved in your heart and try to love the questions themselves.
(Rainer Maria Rilke, adapted)

Reflecting on this week:
> What did you discover this week in the quest of following your
>> questions?
> Are there new questions that now rest in your heart?
> What did your questioning teach you?
> How does all this nurture hope in you?

Pondering . . . Dormant and Fallow

I am listening to the season of contemplation...I am listening to all that lies fallow beneath the earth...I am listening to the sacred winter rest.
(Macrina Wiederkehr, OSB)

> What does it mean for you to be dormant, be at rest, lay fallow?
> How does the season of winter teach you the fruitfulness of rest?
> What helps you to stop the harried-ness of life?
> In what parts of your life might God be calling you to a fallow
>> time?

Be attentive this week to periods of rest...then listen to the sacred grow in you.

There's a certain slant of light, winter afternoons
that oppresses like the heft of cathedral tunes —

— Emily Dickinson

Those of us who suffer from some degree of seasonal affective disorder know very well how November bears down on us. The days grow shorter and the reversal of Daylight Saving Time transforms the ever-earlier twilight into a blue-grey mist. Bright red and yellow leaves have fallen to the ground, where they fade to slick, damp brown.

I crave quiet, and solitude. I want to read, ponder, and listen to music. I desire to be a fallow field under a steely November sky, because only in quietude can I be renewed and revitalized. The cold ground holds the seed safe, waiting for springtime. I know that my early winter is a season to be savored, as all the seasons are to be savored.

Yet I already long for the renewal of April.

Now the green blade riseth from the buried grain,
wheat that in the dark earth many days has lain;
love lives again, that with the dead has been:
Love is come again like wheat that springeth green.

– John MacLeod Campbell Crum

Periods of dormancy can be hard for a 57-year-old "Type A" personality, like me, who's never stopped moving during the waking hours of his time on earth. But God laughs at people who make plans. Last summer, after a freak accident imposed six weeks of dormancy upon me and scuttled most of my plans for an even longer period, God and I had lots of time to laugh together at my situation.

At first, I didn't think it would be that way. But then my wife nursed and comforted me. People visited and prayed for me. Clergy delivered communion. The children in my church's Vacation Bible School sent me the dearest hand-made get well card that still brings tears to my eyes when I look at it by my office phone.

Don't get me wrong. I still wish that the accident never happened. But during times of quiet reflection, as I began the healing process and ever since, I cherish the positive sides of my fallow period. Love did indeed live again, even through the toughest times, and I thank God for revealing that to me.

January 28

> *No human being ever learns to live until he has awakened*
> *to the dormant powers within him.*
>
> —William James

What can I learn from you, mid March morning?
Winter's white velvet cloak has given way to mounds of sooty gray,
melting, like the roadside ruins of some forgotten fairytale kingdom.
Squeals of children, cheeks pinched red by the cold, are silenced,
replaced by the singular song of a lone robin
on an exploratory mission for signs of welcome.
What can I learn from you, early June noontime?
Teasing us with a taste of summer.
The pinks and purples of azaleas have faded,
making room for winking black-eyed susans and majestic roses.
Restless children wriggling in their seats,
eager for the freedom just a few, but oh so far, weeks away.

What can I learn from you, late August afternoon?
The grass is seared brown and the thirsty flowers
humbled under relentless heat are bowing low,
a final curtain call to their adoring audience.
A straw, searching for the last bit of lemonade,
sounds the distress call: "Reinforcements needed, Mom."
What can I learn from you, early December dawn?
The red and yellows of autumn's fiery forests have fallen,
leaving bones of branches etched against a steel gray sky.
Cherubs have replaced the hooligans
who tore up the yard playing football,
and Salvation Army bells gives the signal:
the race down the slippery slope to the holidays has begun.

What can I learn from you, end of season, time of waiting?
Intermission. When God changes the scenery between the acts
of his ageless masterpiece. What do I miss when I linger too long
over the last flowers of summer, or look ahead too eagerly
to the splendor of spring? I miss the beauty that comes in stillness,
the stillness that comes in waiting.
If only I have the wisdom and patience to wait.

> *Lo, the winter is past...the time of the singing of birds is come....*
>
> — Song of Solomon 2:11-12

The comparison between a tree's dormancy in winter and the times when one's spiritual life appears to be stalled has become trite precisely because it is so apt. The growth that is taking place is hidden and invisible, and is often forgotten. Winter dormancy and spiritual inactivity is an analogy that has been helpful to me for years.

Recently, however, I have been thinking of spiritual dormancy as analogous to the simmering process in cooking. For some foods, simmering is a necessary part of preparation, allowing flavors and seasonings to blend and meats to become tender.

The simmering process is sustained by both liquid and heat. So also our spiritual lives need to be immersed in the liquids of prayer and scripture and heated by the fire of the Spirit. It is our openness and attentiveness to the simmering of God's continuing presence and action in our lives that infuses the full flavor of our spiritual growth.

Winter is the time for comfort, for good food and warmth, for the touch of a friendly hand and for a talk beside the fire: it is the time for home.

— Edith Sitwell

A deep, wintery-white snow blankets everything in sight, its beauty silencing the world and my busy self. Housebound by Mother Nature's gift, I delight in unfettered time where stoking the fire, cooking a meal, and reading with abandon replaces the cacophony of phones, faxes, and fellow workers. I walk joyfully in knee-deep snow and shake laden branches, covering myself in a light, delicate snow shower of my own making. In concert with children all over the city, I listen for school closings, cancelled events, weather forecasts, yearning for yet another day at home, another day of quiet existence living the way God wants me to, tranquilly, peacefully. And through it all a dormant child awakes remembering snow castles, snow angels, snowmen...the simple pleasures of yesteryear.

Where has that childlike person gone? Does she lie fallow within her sixty-five year old self? Does it take God's grace within each delicate, lacy, snowflake to summon her ten-year-old spirit? What life messages are to be found within the confines of a record-breaking storm? And will these lessons be remembered when winter turns to spring, and spring to summer?

Echoes of . . . Dormant and Fallow

I am listening to the season of contemplation...I am listening to all that lies fallow beneath the earth...I am listening to the sacred winter rest.
(Macrina Wiederkehr, OSB)

Reflecting back on these days:
    How were you more a human "being" and less a human "doing'?
    What did you learn about your own pace of life?
    Where do you need more fallow space in your life?
    How does all this nurture hope in you?

Pondering . . . Hiddenness

May we learn to trust the goodness of what we cannot see. May we have the courage to visit the frozen ground of our lives, believing in the life that is hidden. (Joyce Rupp)

So much growth is hidden in the earth in winter.
    What hopes rest hidden in your heart?
    What seeds are sleeping in the depths of your being?
    What roots your heart?
    What seeds within you crave to sprout forth from
      their hiddenness?

This week take a walk on the frozen ground outside. Let the heartbeat of the earth resonate with your own heartbeat. Let the earth reveal to you the miracle hidden within it.

In spiritual listening, we encounter a God who cannot be fully understood, we discover realities that cannot be controlled, and we realize that our hope is hidden not in the possession of power, but in the confession of weakness.

— Henri J.M. Nouwen

Only when fate has dealt us an unkind blow, and the rug is pulled out from under us, can we begin to acknowledge that our power to control the events of our lives is limited. Even when the crisis has passed, we often return to our illusion of power and control because any other possibility is a little too scary. Our true Reality remains hidden from our consciousness in the service of our ego.

Henri Nouwen, in the passage above, as well as many mystics of varied traditions, offer their discovered Truth that prayerful listening opens up radical new understandings of who we are and whose world this really is. What's to be noted, however, is that this recognition of our limitations and weaknesses is not just a brave reckoning with Truth or "how things are," but actually a state of grace in which our hope resides. How can this be? Weakness is better than strength – vulnerability preferable to invincibility? The paradox can only be resolved by understanding that by allowing ourselves to be vulnerable and undefended, we open ourselves to God's love and will for our lives. We can then, and only then, let God's Spirit flow through us for the benefit of God's purpose for our world.

Your ego will not like this message. A hundred objections will arise. The Truth is to be found in prayerful listening.

It's extraordinary how we go through life with eyes half shut, with dull ears, with dormant thoughts.

– Joseph Conrad

I have a girlfriend I call over and over again, week after week. Usually, I get her voice mail or she's too busy to talk. Every so often, I get frustrated and feel insecure about the relationship. The friendship seems one-sided. But then, she and I will get together for lunch, and she'll say what a good friend I am. She'll talk about how she misses me. And, all of my feelings of insecurity melt away. For although the relationship may have appeared non-existent, it was merely hidden – dormant for the time being, like the plants underground in winter.

Sometimes we look out the window, especially on a February day, and cannot fathom that, in God's precious time, the dreary landscape will be transformed. But then, come spring, it happens: that magical change. And, we almost breathe a sigh of relief as we relish in the newness – a little surprised that it has happened. Faith is like that. We walk around sometimes with little or no emotion; we simply do what we have to do to make it through the day. We question friendships, wonder about our futures, and muddle through. We often feel insecure and alone. But then, something (sometimes very small) gives us a sign – a glimpse of hope. We remember that God is with us. And our true friends are always there. And that life, with all of its uncertainty and hidden stages, is good. And we begin to feel alive again.

Reach high, for stars lie hidden in your soul.

— Pamela Vaull Starr

Those places within ourselves where we venture not,
the answers we never question
because the questions we never ask, our undiscovered dreams:
so much we keep hidden.

Often, what we hide is what we fear.
Our inadequacies and doubts,
our faults and flaws – we want to remove
these from view. We bury our banes, but still God sees.

We fear our potential, our own possibilities, and these, too, we
obscure. We conceal our capabilities, but still God sees.

And still God loves. And hopes. And waits.

Our best selves squirm in the hiddenness
that we mistake for a haven.
There, banished blessings risk becoming burdens.
All that God sees, loves, hopes and waits for–
that we must nurture, that we must embrace.
Mustering the courage to confront our imperfections
and to course our imaginations,
we reveal our reveries.

We need nothing more than what we hold hidden: may it be holy.

> *Trust that the treasure we look for is hidden in the ground on which we stand.*
>
> — Henri Nouwen

During my life, I attended Sunday school, read Scripture and served in a variety of ministries. But I never really prayed outside of worship, grace before meals, and times of concern for another. On the night of my mother's death, though, I witnessed prayer of a kind I had never even imagined. After the doctor told her that he could do no more, my mother told me that she wanted to pray. What I saw captivated me, as I watched what I can only describe as a communion between Spirit and soul. It left me wondering and hoping for the same. But unlike my mother, I had no idea how to encounter that hidden God to whom she so lovingly surrendered.

In the following months, I read all that I could about prayer, thinking that if I tried hard enough, I could find that for which I hoped. One day, I lay down on a hill, frustrated and ready to give up. I don't know if I slept, but I felt a presence that I somehow knew to be the Spirit. It was neither seen nor heard, but it left in my mind the sense that I had been held, wrapped in a brilliance that enfolded me. I was completely vulnerable to it, but felt no fear. I don't know how long I remained there. But I knew that the Spirit was present and that I was known and loved.

God's presence surrounds us. May we surrender to the hidden embrace.

*Love writes a transparent calligraphy, so on the empty page,
my soul can read and recollect.*

— Rumi

Among the ninety-nine beautiful names for God in the Qur'an is Al-Batin, or "The Hidden One." Having long experienced hiddenness as absence, I was graced by this teaching. If a beloved name for the Divine is "The Hidden," might God offer this attribute to invite us more fully into the presence? I began to reflect on the lessons of hidden-ness.

When I cannot readily sense the presence of the Divine through familiar practices or channels such as my daily prayer or reading, a dryness sets in. During these times, I often experience what the great poets of the spiritual life have described as a hunger, a thirst, even a physical pain. But this longing –however much akin to suffering– is also an awakening. Unable to sense the Divine in familiar ways, I am invited to open other ways of sensing and knowing the presence. When I accept this invitation, hiddenness becomes a pathway for spiritual growth. Only when I feel the pain of longing, can my soul read the transparent words written by a hidden Love.

Echoes of . . . Hiddenness

May we learn to trust the goodness of what we cannot see. May we have the courage to visit the frozen ground of our lives, believing in the life that is hidden.
(Joyce Rupp)

Looking back on this week,
    What hidden hopes did you discover within you?
    How were you invited to deepen your roots?
        ... to uncover new growth?
    What do you see now that you could not see before?
    How does all this nurture hope in you?

Pondering . . . Patience

Trust in the slow work of God.
(Pierre Teilhard de Chardin)

What are the "winter places" in your heart that seem
    very slow to grow?
Where do you most need the grace of patience in your life?
What can the slow work of winter teach you about patience?

This week, look for small signs of life coming from the frozen earth.
Spend time with that small spark of life. Let it teach you patient trust.

*Be patient enough to live one day at a time, letting
yesterday go and leaving tomorrow until it arrives.*

— Unknown

My niece, a new young mother of a delightful little boy with a mild
form of autism, has developed into a beautiful, strong, and patient
woman. She spends a great deal of time working with her son to meet
the demands of his disability, never making him feel different, but
rather very special. Even though the risk of having another child with
autism exists, she has a desire to have more children. This led her to
have another cyst (one of many) removed to pave the way for a preg-
nancy in the very near future. This kind of patient love is so inspiring
to me. My niece is well aware of her chances, but her deep love of the
life she and her husband have created has surpassed that fear.

We spend a great deal of our lives worrying about things over which
we have no control. How much more at peace we could be if we just
patiently put our concerns into the hands of our God who is always
there, patiently waiting for us to share what lies within our hearts. It
is not up to me or to any of us to tell God what we want to happen.
Instead greater peace will be ours if we accept and believe that God
who loves us is always there for us.

Patience is a necessary ingredient of genius.

— Benjamin Disraeli

Patience truly is a necessary ingredient of genius. As an art historian, when I think of this quote by Benjamin Disraeli, I think of Michelangelo. It confounds me how he took a block of marble, and would, as he himself wrote, "liberate the figure imprisoned in the marble." What extraordinary patience and genius to be able to visualize a figure and spend years, sometimes decades, to see it finished. And his figures, such as those of David and Moses, are colossal, many times larger than life, making it even more stunning. Then there is, of course, the Sistine Chapel. The artist worked for Pope Julius II, who was impatient to see it finished; but Michelangelo was determined to execute the entire project alone, and, in four years, he did. What patience, what determination, what genius, and what an extraordinary result!

Adopt the pace of nature; her secret is patience.

— Ralph Waldo Emerson

Yesterday it was just a shaded, cold, barren woods
That lay outside my window
And just like today there were no leaves
Dangling from the hands of branches
No glorious fall or spring colors on display
And just like today the wind was blowing
And the air had a nasty bitterness in her breath

But yesterday was before
The snowflakes of last night
Yesterday was before
The blanket which now lay upon the ground
And the cotton now stuck
To the arms of trees

Yesterday was before the children's footprints
And the tracks of sleds
Were brushes on the canvas
Yesterday was before the snowmen,
And the snow fights and the cups of cocoa

Yesterday was before
A mother's breath on a kitchen window
Eyes looking outward...

Yet my eyes,
My eyes drift inward
At the barren woods,
Shaded and cold
At the barren branches
Hoping for color

And pray tonight for snowflakes.

Maintain...the Center.

— Lao Tzu

This past April, I was fully immersed in life. David, my son, was hospitalized for over three weeks with pneumonia, and because of an underlying medical condition, he required a temporary tracheotomy. The "trach" prevented him from speaking, which required him to communicate with pen and paper. His frustration was apparent, and for my wife and me, a very painful experience and reminder of the unspeakable.

During David's hospital stay, my father, who had been suffering from Alzheimer's, died. In between daily visits to the hospital, we managed to squeeze in a funeral.

Throughout this period, faith and focus enabled me to observe these life experiences from a vortex, but with David home (and doing well) and my father buried, I find my "faith/focus" diffused.

Where is my center now? I feel disconnected from my spiritual life. How might I regain my connectivity to the Great Source? I am inclined to try to force myself back into relationship, but I know that such effort would be met with my own willful frustration.

It occurs to me that my spiritual relationship is a dual one. I am one half of the equation; the other half of my relationship reminds me that during times of spiritual drought I must "Be still and know that I am God!"

So I sit, wait, and contemplate the stillness.

Patience is a virtue.

– ancient proverb

Some of my earliest memories are of hearing my Mother quote this proverb to me. I remember marveling at how she could sit unraveling my yarn and picking up the dropped stitches of childhood knitting projects. All through life I have wanted to hurry on to the next step, the next stage. And then God sent me a child who was a "dawdler," always late to leave for school or any activity.

As I have struggled with "patience" through a long lifetime, I have come to believe that it equates with acceptance – acceptance of life's irritations and limitations. Patience can smooth adolescent turmoil as well as the losses of aging. Patience fosters endurance which breeds strength, and ultimately courage.

I need to remember that I can claim God's strength at any time, for any situation when my own strength is exhausted. The fact that I hit every red light when I am running late can be a time of gratitude and prayerful thoughts.

God is not finished with any of us yet, so don't give up on the incomplete you and me. We'll be patient.

Echoes of . . . Patience

Trust in the slow work of God.
(Pierre Teilhard de Chardin)

As you reflect on these days,
How did you experience the slow work of God within your heart?
What did patience teach you this week?
What did winter teach you of patience?
How does all this nurture hope in you?

Pondering . . . Resilience

In the depths of winter, I finally learned that within me there lay an invincible summer.
(Camus)

How have you experienced your own resilience?
How have those times transformed you?
What images does this word bring to mind for you?
Where in your heart do you need the strength of resilience?

This week, be aware of ways that God brings forth an "invincible summer" and renews your strength in the midst of pitfalls and uncertainties.

When we are anchored in the peace of God, outer change cannot disturb the integrity of our soul.

—Alan Cohen

There are times when adversity shakes us to our core, uprooting us from life as we know it. Often, we discover an inner strength of which we were unaware, granting us grace, endurance, and flexibility to move through difficulty. God's deep peace anchors us amidst the chaos.

One need only observe nature to be reminded of the surprising gift of resilience. Last winter, I found myself regularly inspired by a tree outside my window. It stood strong against the blizzard winds and heavy snows of our historic winter. Sustained by its hidden root system, the tree not only withstood the storms, it offered food and shelter to the birds.

Like the tree, we have a root system that sustains us in tough times. However, too often we neglect it. For a long time, I looked for God "out there," not realizing that God was closer than I imagined. Since I have discovered and begun tending the God-life buried within me, I have experienced a deeper sense of strength and peace. This soul work, done with the assistance of others, helps me live with integrity.

There is a deep source of life within each of us that wants–that needs– to be tended.

Do not let what you cannot do interfere with what you can do.

— John Wooden

The gentle snow reminds me of the power of waiting:
that change comes in its own time;
that it can be both beautiful and treacherous.
That big things can happen when we work together –
like landscapes transformed,
snowflake upon snowflake.

The snow-draped evergreen reminds me to stand tall,
holding my burdens lightly.
Strong and true, looking heavenward,
sure that God is with me in this time of transformation.

The grass reminds me to bear the weight of others gently.
To welcome change,
for often in change lies great beauty.
To wait silently, patiently,
through the dark, cold winter,
for the new birth of spring.

So let me not forget the lessons of the winter snow:
silence, patience, beauty, peacefulness,
transformation, resilience, waiting . . .
For these are lessons worth pondering.

He's a million rubber bands in his resilience.

— Alan K. Simpson

We might not recognize Simpson's name, but we all can recognize the type of resilience to which he refers. The best and strongest rubber band can be stretched and stretched until it successfully accomplishes the job which it was meant to do – holding things together securely. The most resilient person can be stretched by life's circumstances, almost to the breaking point. Yet, like a strong rubber band, she or he does not break, but instead successfully holds it all together. Imagine then, a person who is like 1,000,000 strong rubber bands! When there are a million rubber bands, even if several of them break, there are many more to hold things together. A person like a million rubber bands faces life realistically, recognizing that he or she is broken in some places. Yet such a person has an inner reserve of strength and determination that communicates to others, "I might have some brokenness in my life, but I am not broken. I use my strengths and talents to overcome those adversities which have been thrust at me, as well as adversities to which I have contributed."

...And then the snow came, we were always out shoveling, and we'd drop to sleep exhausted. Then we'd wake up, and it's snowing....

— Dar Williams

I love the snow. I also love winter. I actually welcome all seasons, but I especially celebrate the arrival of winter. If I listen to newscasters in the winter, I'm in the minority. An anticipated blustery day or blizzard produces warnings about bundling up or stocking up. Yet I rejoice!

I believe that winter is God's way of slowing us down. The warmth of fireplaces, a cozy thick sweater, curling up with a book, or watching football with friends.... all are wintry treasures to me. And that occasional blizzard? I smile as the whole region stands still. We have excuses NOT to go somewhere. Our family gathers in one place, and remains there, at least for a while. The snow makes everything beautiful, and quiet. Pure peace.

Yes, we must shovel. But for me, snow is a break from the routine of a busy life. It restores me. I take a breath and I take a moment. I am awed by the wonder of nature. I learn from the resilience of bent tree limbs as well as from my tired muscles after shoveling. We bounce back, especially at home, surrounded by those we love.

Promise me you'll always remember:
You're braver than you believe, and stronger than you seem,
and smarter than you think.

— A.A. Milne

Where does resilience begin?
It begins in prayer.
When life crowds in upon you
And it is difficult to breathe
Remember the Giver and Sustainer
Is waiting to hear from you
And will answer when you call.

When all else fails
When the pressure is too high
And the strength is too low
When the questions are too hard
And the answers nowhere to be found
Where does one go?
To whom does one go?

Back to the beginning
To the Source of Life
Humbly, with bowed head
And bended knee
For what begins and sustains the inner journey
The journey to our true self
Is prayer.

But what of unanswered prayer?
Ah, the true essence of resilience
Believing that God is listening and working on our behalf,
Even when it appears otherwise.
Resilience is trusting in the ultimate outcome
Trusting that God is present and working
Even when we feel very alone.

Echoes of . . . Resilience

In the depths of winter, I finally learned that within me there lay an invincible summer.
(Camus)

Recalling this past week,
 How did you experience your own resilience?
 What new strength have you discovered within you?
 Where did you find your "invincible summer"?
 How does all this nurture hope in you?

Pondering . . . Shelter and Sanctuary

I love you, O God, my strength. You are my rock and my fortress, a safe shelter in whom I see refuge.
(Psalm 18:1-2)

All of us need "safe places" in our lives.
 Where do you "take shelter" in times of need and struggle?
 Who are those who offer you "sanctuary" in their hearts?
 How are you a sanctuary or shelter for others?

This week, take some quiet time to pray in gratitude for those in your life who have been a safe shelter for you. Perhaps even write them a note of thanks!

O Lord, support us all the day long, until the shadows lengthen, and the evening comes, and the busy world is hushed, and the fever of life is over, and our work is done, then in thy mercy, grant us a safe lodging, and a holy rest, and peace at the last.

— Book of Common Prayer

We all have cherished memories of safe places from our childhood. One of mine is a "fort," built out of blankets, sheets and pillows. I'd crawl inside with a flashlight and feel secure and protected. The fort was a "safe lodging and a place of rest," waiting for me when I came home from school.

Seeking and finding shelter is not so different as an adult. The places change but the feelings remain the same. Now, I find shelter in the embrace of my husband's arms, sitting in my church sanctuary surrounded by beautiful stained glass windows, and with my weekly spiritual education group. I feel "at home" and sense God's presence with these people and in these places.

Shelter is commonly described as a refuge or something that offers protection. Psalm 91 express this well, "You who live in the shelter of the Most High, who abide in the shadow of the Almighty, will say to the Lord, 'My refuge and my fortress; my God, in whom I trust.'" Shelter is always present, when we seek our refuge in God.

Even before the rabbit had gotten herself tucked in, a fox trotted up to the mitten, and after a good deal of trouble, she got herself in along with the others. The mouse was beginning to think that maybe she shouldn't have been so generous, but with the bitter wind outside, what else could she do?

— folktale, retold by Alvin Tresselt

One winter, I experienced my own bitter wind: an inability to stop drinking, even for one day. After being sheltered in jails and institutions for a few years, I was still hopelessly incapable of staying sober and needed sanctuary from a disease that was killing me. Although I'd wandered in and out of the rooms of Alcoholics Anonymous, I was uncommitted to surrendering my will and life to the care of God. In a state of darkness, I doubted God's love for me, even the very existence of a Higher Power that could heal me. I'd reached bottom.

Then my miracle happened. I opened up to the possibility that my fellow alcoholics in the rooms of AA could be my sanctuary, just like the fox had found sanctuary with the other forest animals in the mitten. By receiving the unexpected grace of their love, hope, and generosity, I realized I could stay warm and safe, at least for one day, by crawling in to a meeting room and allowing myself to be protected. And one winter day, that's just what I did.

Since then, I've learned to stay sober a day at a time. From other alcoholics, I learned the power of God's ever-present love and forgiveness. There are still times when I feel the bitter winds and shiver in darkness, but now I can choose to seek shelter in the protection and grace of God.

*Every dreamer knows that it is entirely possible to be
homesick for a place you've never been too, perhaps more
homesick than for familiar ground.*

— Judith Thurman

Thoughts of sanctuary often conjure up images of a safe haven, a restful retreat from the stresses, worries, and anxieties of this busy world; a serene and protective shelter from storms. In winter, many crave sanctuary to rest the soul and spirit, to sink into the nourishing darkness that is nature's resting time, and lie fallow. I need that –all of it– to regain wholeness.

But sometimes, in contrast, I need a bright, vibrant, energetic sanctuary to escape the heaviness and worries of the world. I need a place of light and joy, of color and laughter, where I can become filled with childlike amazement for all of life. This exuberant sanctuary sometimes flows from the serene, protective environment of the soul's winter.

I have become aware that I can choose this vibrant sanctuary just as easily as the quiet shelter. I need and want both in my life in order to live as the whole, creative, and loving person that God calls me to be. Today, I choose the vibrant, energetic sanctuary of my studio, where I will immerse myself in color and texture. I will smile as I let go of the woes of the world and create a new thing, which refreshes me in the process. Ah! Off to my exuberant sanctuary!

What kind of sanctuary do you need today?

Lord prepare me to be a sanctuary.

— John W. Thompson and Randy Scruggs

My deepest experiences of shelter have been with the Lord in prayer during my greatest times of despair. When my heart knows of no way out of a problem and calls out for the Holy One for help, God mysteriously and gently lifts me from the dark place and brings me to the safe harbor, a place I cannot conjure up on my own. It is the ultimate sanctuary.

It is in this sacred place that I find this sacred truth: when I am living into God's call for me in my life, I am guaranteed the safety for which I crave. When I look for shelter elsewhere, it is anything but safe. My home and true shelter are found in the inner sanctuary of my soul, joined by the Spirit of God.

The King of love my shepherd is,
whose goodness faileth never;
I nothing lack if I am his, and he is mine forever.

And so through all the length of days
thy goodness faileth never;
Good Shepherd, may I sing thy praise
within thy house forever.

— Henry Williams Baker

Do you remember building forts? My brothers and I would drag all the blankets and sheets off our beds, and set up elaborate tents using beds, chairs, sofas, chests, bookcases – anything we could move in our rooms or the "playroom," as we called it in the sixties. Mom had a fit every time, but it never stopped us. I guess the urge was too great to build a place of shelter, a secret place, a hidden world. Sometimes the fort was for loud and silly games. At other times, it was a place to hide, read, be alone with our thoughts, a sanctuary. I still feel safe just thinking about it.

Now that I'm grown, I still seek a safe place now and then. Sometimes it's a physical space, but not always. I know now that I can find that safe feeling when I pray either with words or with song. My conversations with God bring me to the sanctuary of hope that abides in me. Songs in my heart and my head bring me the gift of peace.

Echoes of . . . Shelter and Sanctuary

I love you, O God, my strength. You are my rock and my fortress, a safe shelter in whom I see refuge.
(Psalm 18:1-2)

As you look back on these days,
> How were you invited to know your God as shelter and strength?
> Where or with whom did you find yourself seeking shelter or sanctuary?
> Where were you invited to be shelter for another?

How has your winter of hope brought you new life?
> What blessings and wisdom has this winter of hope brought your way?
> How has winter hope nourished your spirit?

Pondering . . . The Gift of Hope

Oh Lord, how shining and festive is your gift to us,
if we only look, and see.
(Mary Oliver)

Every day is a gift . . . this year we get an added gift!
How will you use it?
How will you live in greater hope and love?

Look and see!

Our own pulse beats…within the flowered ground beneath our feet… We can hear it in water, in wood, and even in stone… We are earth of this earth, and we are bone of its bone. This is a prayer I sing…

— Barbara Deming

My friend Kathy and I waded, pruning shears in hand, along the stream coursing through my lower meadow. We were clearing overhanging brush, working and chattering happily under the mid-summer sun. In an instant, we were drawn to a glint of iridescence on the stream bank: a trio of damsel flies hovered just above the grasses. Never having witnessed this intricate mating dance, we stood transfixed, barely whispering our sense of awe. Time expanded; we felt the chill of the stream water; we breathed the aroma of the sun-warmed leaves and grasses. We were still. It was beauty that invited us to this stillness, and it was grace that held us in its embrace. Neither of us knows exactly how long we stood there—maybe thirty minutes, maybe an hour. The refreshment, however, lingers to this day each time I recall the gift of those moments when we, most certainly, knew the presence of God.

In Gratitude

A large, dedicated group of people, listed below, came together to bring this book to life. These friends of Well for the Journey offered their time, talent, and enthusiasm to make this dream a reality. It has been a great pleasure and a real honor to work with everyone associated with the production of this book.

-Kathy Baker

Franklin Adkinson
Jeff Ayres
Barbara Bachur
Virginia Barnhart
Donna Bilek
Mimi Bourgeois
Karen Brown
Mitchell Brown
Tina Brown
JoAnn Burke
Annette Chappell
Greg Cochran
Sutton Dischinger
Cheryl Duvall
Caroline Ellison
Patricia Fosarelli
John Frisch
Robert Glushakow
Caroline Gonya
Kerry Graham
Rebekah Hatch
Mabeth Hudson
JungGeum Im
Elaine Ireland
Lori Lucas

Pamela McGinnis
Cathy McNally
Kathy McNany
Debbie McQuillen
Avidan Milevsky
Donna Mollenkopf
Courtney Muller
Leland Nislow
Margaret Petersen
Anne Pidcock
Mari Quint
Whitney Ransome
Amy Schmaljohn
Peggy Shouse
Becky Slater
Scott Slater
Bob Smith
Grace Smith
Terri Smith
Susan Saunders
Anne Sonntag
Sandy Towers
Bruce Wilson
Jane Woltereck
Doris Zimmerman

Works Cited

November 30 – December 6

Richardson, Jan L. *Night Visions: Searching the Shadows of Advent and Christmas*. Cleveland: Pilgrim Press,1998.

Holy Bible. Akron: Ivy Books, 1991. (canticle version used)

Morneau, Robert F. *Songs Out of Silence: 99 Sayings by Jessica Powers (99 Words to Live By)*. First edition ed. East Providence: New City Press, 2010.

The Holy Bible: New Revised Standard Version with Apocrypha. Text ed. New York: Oxford University Press, USA, 1991.

The Holy Bible: New Revised Standard Version with Apocrypha. Text ed. New York: Oxford University Press, USA, 1991.

Shaia, Alexander and Michelle Gaugy. *The Hidden Power of the Gospels: Four Questions, Four Paths, One Journey*. New York: Harperone, 2010.

Richardson, Jan L. *Night Visions: Searching the Shadows of Advent and Christmas*. Cleveland: Pilgrim Press,1998.

December 7 – 13

Good News Bible: With Deuterocanonicals /Apochrypha. New York: American Bible Society, 1992.

Etz Hayim: Torah and Commentary. Philadelphia: Jewish Publication Society Of America, 2001.

Eskenazi, Tamara Cohn, ed. and Andrea Weiss, ed. *The Torah: A Women's Commentary*. Albany: Urj Press, 2007.

Parker, Philip M. *Prayer – Webster's Quotations, Facts and Phrases*. San Diego: Icon Group International, 2008.

The Holy Bible: English Standard Version (Classic Pew and Worship Edition, Black). Wheaton: Crossway Bibles, 2003.

Roberts, Lee. *The NKJV UltraSlim Bible*. Waco: Thomas Nelson, 1999.

Sarton, Mary. /hubpages.com/hub/AIDS-by-Mary-Sarton (accessed August 16, 2010)

Good News Bible: With Deuterocanonicals /Apochrypha. New York: American Bible Society, 1992.

December 14 – 20

Touber,Tinj. http://www.odemagazine.com/doc/55/because-god-whispers (accessed August 14, 2010).

Disraeli, Benjamin. Tancred Vol. 1: Or, The New Crusade. Charleston: Bibliobazaar, 2007.

Holy Bible: New Revised Standard Version with Apocrypha. Text Ed. New York: Oxford University Press, USA, 1991.

Hall, Sr. Jeremy. *Silence, Solitude, Simplicity*. Collegeville: Liturgical Press, 2007.

Gately, Edwina. I*n God's Womb: A Spiritual Memoir.* Maryknoll: Orbis Books, 2009.

Spoto, Donald. *In Silence: Why We Pray.* New York: Penguin Group, 2004.

Touber,Tinj. http://www.odemagazine.com/doc/55/because-god-whispers (accessed August 14, 2010).

December 21 – 27

O'Donohue, John. *To Bless the Space Between Us: A Book of Blessings*. New York: Doubleday Broadway Publishing, 2008.

Howe, Edgar Watson. http://www.landofwisdom.com/author/edgar-watson-howe/page5.html (accessed August 14, 2010).

Oliver, Mary. *New and Selected Poems, Volume One*. Boston: Beacon Press, 1992.

Peterson, Wilferd Arlan. *The Art of Living: Thoughts on Meeting the Challenge of Life*. New York: Galahad Books, 1993.

Ortega y Gasset, Jose. *The Revolt of the Masses.* New York: W.W. Norton and Company, 1993.

Niles, John Jacob. www.lyricsmania.com/i_wonder_as_i_wander_lyrics_christmas_songs.html (accessed August 14, 2010)

O'Donohue, John. *To Bless the Space Between Us: A Book of Blessings*. New York, NY: Doubleday Broadway Publishing, 2008.

December 28 – January 3

Rowe, David D. and Robert Schulmann. *Einstein on Politics: His Private Thoughts and Public Stands on Nationalism, Zionism, War, Peace and The Bomb.* Princeton: Princeton University Press, 2007.

The 1979 Book of Common Prayer. New York: Oxford University Press, 2005.

Wiederkehr, Macrina. *Seasons of Your Heart: Prayers and Reflections, Revised and Expanded.* New York, NY: Harper Collins Publishers, 1991.

O'Donohue, John. *Anam Cara: A Book of Celtic Wisdom*. New York: Harper Collins Publishers, 1997.

Stevens, Wallace. *The Collected Poems of Wallace Stevens*. New York: Vintage Books, 1990.

Mogul, Wendy. *Blessings of a Skinned Knee: Using Jewish Teachings to Raise Self-Reliant Children*. New York: PenguinPutnam, Inc., 2001.

Rowe, David D. and Robert Schulmann. *Einstein on Politics: His Private Thoughts and Public Stands on Nationalism, Zionism, War, Peace and The Bomb*. Princeton: Princeton University Press, 2007.

January 4 – 10

Peterson, Eugene H. *The Message: Numbered Edition*. Colorado Springs: NavPress Publishing Group, 2005.

Jagger, Mick and Richards, Keith. www.lyricsdomain.com/18/rolling_stones/you_cant_always_get_what_you_want.html (accessed August 15, 2010)

De Saint-Exupery, Antoine. *Wind, Sand and Stars*. New York: Harvest Books, 2002.

Animal Collective. www.absolutelyrics.com/lyrics/view/animal_collective/kids_on_holiday (accessed August 15, 2010).

Danielson, Annie. thestudio.danielsondesigns.com (accessed August 15, 2010).

Basho, Matsuo. *Narrow Road to the Interior: And Other Writings (Shambhala Classics)*. New ed. Boston: Shambhala, 2000.

Peterson, Eugene H. *The Message: Numbered Edition*. Colorado Springs: NavPress Publishing Group, 2005.

January 11 – 17

Sullivan, K. D. *A Cure For The Common Word*. 1 ed. New York: McGraw-Hill, 2007.

Kidd, Sue Monk. *When the Heart Waits: Spiritual Direction for Life's Sacred Questions*. San Francisco: HarperSanFrancisco, 1992.

Nouwen, Henri J.M. *The Path Of Waiting*. New York: Crossroad Publishing Company, 1995.

The Holy Bible: New Revised Standard Version with Apocrypha. Text ed. New York: Oxford University Press, USA, 1991.

Ortberg, John. *If You Want to Walk on Water, You've Got to Get Out of the Boat*. Grand Rapids: Zondervan, 2001.

Brueggemann, Walter. *Awed to Heaven, Rooted in Earth: Prayers of Walter Brueggemann*. Minneapolis: Augsburg Fortress Publishers, 2003.

Sullivan, K. D. *A Cure For The Common Word*. 1 ed. New York: McGraw-Hill, 2007.

January 18 – 24

Rilke, Rainer Maria. *Letters to a Young Poet*. 2nd ed. Novato: New
    World Library, 2000.

Bach, Richard. *Running from Safety: An Adventure of the Spirit*. New
    York: Delta, 1995.

Rumi, Jelaluddin. *The Essential Rumi*. Ed. Coleman Barks. London: Penguin
    Books Ltd, 2004.

Calaprice, Alice, Freeman Dyson, and Albert Einstein. *New Quotable Einstein*.
    Princeton: Princeton University Press, 2005.

Gardner, John W. *Self-Renewal: The Individual and the Innovative Society*.
    New York: W. W. Norton & Company, 1995.

Catholic Comparative New Testament. New York: Oxford University
    Press, 2005.

Rilke, Rainer Maria. *Letters to a Young Poet*. 2nd ed. Novato: New World
    Library, 2000.

January 25 – 31

Rupp, Joyce, and Macrina Wiederkehr. *The Circle Of Life: The Heart's
    Journey Through The Seasons*. Notre Dame: Sorin Books, 2005.

Johnson, Emily and Thomas H. *The Complete Poems of Emily Dickinson*.
    Boston: Little Brown, 1961.

Crum, John MacLeod Campbell. *Hymnal 1982 According to the Use of the
    Episcopal Church*. New York: Church Publishing, 1985.

James, William. thinkexist.com/search/searchquotationasp?search=
    dormant (accessed August 15, 2010)

Holy Bible. King James Version. Reissue ed. New York: Plume, 1974.

Sitwell, Edith. www.goodreads.com/author/quotes/65646.Edith_
    Sitwell (accessed August 15, 2010)

Rupp, Joyce, and Macrina Wiederkehr. *The Circle Of Life: The Heart's
    Journey Through The Seasons*. Notre Dame: Sorin Books, 2005.

February 1 – 7

Rupp, Joyce, and Macrina Wiederkehr. *The Circle Of Life: The Heart's
    Journey Through The Seasons*. Notre Dame: Sorin Books, 2005.

Nouwen, Henri J. M. Spiritual Direction: *Wisdom for the Long Walk of Faith*.
    New York: HarperOne, 2006.

Conrad, Joseph. *Lord Jim (Oxford World's Classics)*. New York: Oxford
    University Press, USA, 2008.

Starr, Pamela Vaull. http://quotationsbook.com/author/6920 (accessed
    August 15, 2010).

Nouwen, Henri J. M. *Bread for the Journey: A Daybook of Wisdom and
    Faith*. New York: HarperOne. 1997.

Rumi, Jelaluddin. *The Essential Rumi.* Ed. Coleman Barks. London: Penguin Books Ltd, 2004.

Rupp, Joyce, and Macrina Wiederkehr. *The Circle Of Life: The Heart's Journey Through The Seasons.* Notre Dame: Sorin Books, 2005.

February 8 – 14

Whitcomb, Holly W. *Seven Spiritual Gifts Of Waiting.* New York: Augsburg Books, 2005.

http://www.coolquotes.com/quotes/unknown.html (accessed August 15, 2010)

Monypenny, William Flavelle. *The Life of Benjamin Disraeli, Earl of Bea consfield (Volume 2).* New York: General Books LLC, 2010.

Emerson, Ralph Waldo. *Selected Writings of Ralph Waldo Emerson (Signet Classics).* 2003. Reprint. New York: Signet Classics, 2003.

Tzu, Lao. *Lao Tzu: Te-Tao Ching - A New Translation Based on the Recently Discovered Ma-wang-tui Texts (Classics of Ancient China).* Chicago: Ballantine Books, 1992.

Titleman, Gregory Y. *Random House Dictionary of Popular Proverbs and Sayings.* New York: Random House, 1996.

Whitcomb, Holly W. Seven Spiritual Gifts Of Waiting. New York: Augsburg Books, 2005.

February 15 – 21

Sherman, David. *Camus (Blackwell Great Minds).* New ed. Malden: Wiley-Blackwell, 2008.

Cohen, Alan. *The Dragon Doesn't Live Here Anymore.* Chicago: Ballantine Books, 1993.

Wooden, John. *They Call Me Coach.* 1 ed. New York: McGraw-Hill, 2003.

Simpson, Alan K. www.brainyquote.com/quotes/keywords/resilience.html (accessed June 2, 2010).

Williams, Dar. www.metrolyrics.com/february-lyrics-dar-williams.html (accessed August 14, 2010).

Milne, A.A. www.landofwisdom.com/author/a-a-milne (accessed August 14, 2010)

Sherman, David. Camus (Blackwell Great Minds). New ed. Malden: Wiley-Blackwell, 2008.

February 22 – 28
Crahan OSB, Sr. Marietta. *The Psalms for Our Daily Prayer.* (translation by the Benedictine Sisters of Perpetual Adoration).

The 1979 Book of Common Prayer. New York: Oxford University Press, USA, 2005.

International Bible Society. *NIV Study Bible, 10th Anniversary Edition.* Colorado Springs, CO: Zondervan, 1995.

Tresselt, Alvin. *The Mitten.* New York: HarperTrophy, 1989.

Thurman, Judith. www.goodreads.com/author/quotes/14851.judith thurman (accessed August 14, 2010).

Thompson, John W. and Randy Scruggs. Worshiparchive.com/song/sanctuary (accessed August 13, 2010).

Baker, Henry Williams. www.hymnsite.com/lyrics/umh138.sht (accessed August 15, 2010).

Crahan OSB, Sr. Marietta. *The Psalms for Our Daily Prayer.* (translation by the Benedictine Sisters of Perpetual Adoration).

February 29
Oliver, Mary. *Why I Wake Early.* Boston: Beacon Press, 2004.

Macy, Joanna R. *Coming Back to Life: Practices to Reconnect Our Lives, Our World.* Gabriola Island: New Society Publishers, 1998.

INDEX OF THEMES